METAPHYSICAL BELIEFS

METAPHYSICAL BELIEFS

Three Essays by

STEPHEN TOULMIN
RONALD W. HEPBURN
ALASDAIR MACINTYRE

with a Preface by Alasdair MacIntyre

SCHOCKEN BOOKS · NEW YORK

First published 1957
This edition, with a new Preface, 1970
© SCM Press Ltd 1970
Printed in Great Britain

CONTENTS

v

III

THE LOGICAL STATUS OF RELIGIOUS BELIEF

by ALASDAIR MACINTYRE, *Lecturer in the Philosophy of Religion in the University of Manchester*

PREFACE TO THE 1970 EDITION

THIS book reflects the intellectual climate in which these essays were originally written, a climate that proved transient. Philosophy in the early fifties in Britain had already left behind for the most part the actual doctrines of logical positivism. Indeed these doctrines were never generally held in that country, although for a time they were widely and rightly influential, especially in the form in which they were represented by Ayer in *Language, Truth and Logic*. But the teaching of Moore and of Russell, the growing influence of Wittgenstein's views, even although these were often presented in a second-hand and derivative way, an increasing awareness of the world of Quine and of Carnap, and in Oxford the personal influence of Austin's work had in fact led not only to an admirable attention to and interest in philosophical detail, but also to a sense rather than an assertion that an interest in anything other than details was of a slightly suspect character. Metaphysics was out, perhaps in part because of the influence of the verification principle, but in part because metaphysical questions were taken to be large questions, and large questions were out. Austin's later declaration that importance is not important, but that truth is, captures very well the earlier unformulated—and sometimes explicitly denied—view that to be interested both in what was true and what was important was at the very least very difficult. There were of course other rather different attitudes at work in British philosophy; but it is certain that something of the sort I have described really existed.

Moreover it was to this that theologians responded when in same period they took it that philosophy was essentially dominated by logical positivism. The philosophy with which theologians were acquainted and to which they were sympathetic tended to be either Thomist or Idealist, and in

vii

any case the revival of biblical theology under the influence both of Barth and of Anglican scholars such as Lightfoot, had indirectly had the effect of turning theologians away from philosophical questions. It was in part the intention of this book to restore dialogue between philosophers and theologians, and whether it had this effect or not dialogue certainly *did* increase and *did* improve in quality. But this might provide a case for *not* reprinting *this* book, especially since the thought of all three writers has developed since. What makes reprinting defensible is not only the evidence of demand since it first fell out of print, but also the fact that each of these essays was and is a contribution to a continuing enterprise.

Stephen Toulmin's concern in his essay in this book was to show how scientific concepts may be illegitimately extended and applied in the interests of myth-making. But his essay demonstrates an independent interest in myth, and his remonstrances at the misuse of scientific concepts were in no way based on a positivistic view of science. Much of his subsequent writing has indeed been occupied with arguing that the positivistic view of science is incompatible with an adequate history of science. He has followed R. G. Collingwood (as also notably has Thomas Kuhn in *The Structure of Scientific Revolutions*) in showing how the construction of scientific theories has in fact grown out of and presupposed larger systems of belief about the nature of the universe and the nature of man. But Toulmin has criticized both Collingwood and Kuhn for the way in which they have characterized this relationship. Both Collingwood and Kuhn have attacked the problem of how the key transitions are made in science, not just from one particular theory to another, but from one whole body of theory to another. Both Collingwood and Kuhn envisage these transitions as concerned with what Collingwood called the 'absolute presuppositions' of an age and Kuhn calls its 'paradigms', that is with a body of beliefs themselves not so much part of science as informing the whole direction and mode of science in their own period. Toulmin has criticized Collingwood for picturing the transition from one set of presuppositions to another as being so sharp and abrupt as to be unintelligible; and he has criticized Kuhn for a false contrast between periods of scientific 'revolution' and periods of normal 'science' (*Conceptual Revolutions in Science* in *Boston Studies in the Philosophy of Science*, Volume III, edited by Cohen and Wartofsky). But how then ought the relationship between scientific theories and these background beliefs to be characterized?

Kuhn has argued that we cannot formulate an independent distinction between metaphysics (understood as the domain of these background beliefs) and science, valid for all times and places, because each metaphysics in this sense involves the formulation of its own version of this distinction. But we can nevertheless distinguish between those metaphysical beliefs which have provided a fertile background for scientific theorizing and those which have not. In the essay in this book Toulmin was concerned not with science as growing out of metaphysics, but with metaphysics growing out of science and in such a way as to be empty of any further stimulus for scientific enquiry. Hence this may be regarded as an early contribution to the impressive historical investigation on which Toulmin is now engaged and in which he aims to show in a number of concrete historical settings how the relationship of metaphysics to science has actually been worked out.

Ronald Hepburn's essay too turned out to be part of larger work in both philosophy of religion and in aesthetics. In both fields Hepburn has concerned himself with one central problem, that of the relationship between the coherence and the creative character of experience on the one hand and such claims to truth as may be made on the other. His work in the present essay was extended in this direction most importantly perhaps in his examination of recent theology in *Christianity and Paradox* and in his essay in *Objections to Humanism*. But although Hepburn's work has been outstandingly important in this direction, there is another problem to which he has applied himself perhaps uniquely, a problem which is also raised in the present essay. This problem can only be posed if one takes, as Hepburn does, a radically sceptical view about the difficulty of making good the claims of theology, whether these are based on appeals to faith, metaphysical argument, historical claims or arguments which appeal to religious experience. Most sceptical writers, when they have, as far as they can see, shown such claims to be baseless, apparently lose all interest in any creative or constructive approach to religion. Hepburn, on the contrary, is deeply concerned with the questions of how the experience of the numinous may continue to play a crucial part in human life and how the religious imagination may even for the intellectually sceptical be kept alive. But Hepburn's present essay, like my own, was part of a continuing discussion. How do matters stand on these issues now?

Hepburn regarded my position in the present essays as one in which 'wild' and even 'daring' manoeuvres are resorted to to preserve the Christian faith when all its usual intellectual bases have been removed. But in fact this position has been ably defended since by D. Z. Phillips (*From God to World?* Aristotelian Soc. Supp. Vol. 1967) and others. Their central contention, like my own in the present essay, has been that religion is a specific 'form of life' with its own criteria, its own methods of settling its own questions. So religion cannot be refuted by those sceptics who employ inappropriate criteria, and who try to dismiss religious beliefs because they would be unsatisfactory were they interpreted as, for example, scientific hypotheses. It is perhaps worth putting on record some of my reasons for dissatisfaction with this position, which I formerly held; I can best exemplify this dissatisfaction by considering the problem of evil. Christian theologians have not merely conceded that the existence of evil in the world constitutes a *prima facie* objection to any belief that the world was created by and is ruled by a god at once omnipotent and benevolent; it is rather part of the core belief of Christianity that God wills to exclude evil from the world, has the power to do so, but has not yet done so. We are therefore in the position that the existence of evil is construed by theologians themselves as *prima facie* evidence against belief in the God of Christian theism. But if this is so, then surely they are treating Christian belief as factual in a perfectly ordinary sense, and if this in turn is so, then surely the contention that the criteria by which Christian belief is to be judged are altogether different from other criteria fails at once. In other words my first reason for abandoning my own earlier position is that I came to see that position as importantly inconsistent with the very professions of that religious faith of which it professed to be the elucidation.

Secondly, and as importantly, I came to see the justice of Hepburn's remarks about wild and daring manoeuvres, above all the justice of the word 'manoeuvres'. For Christianity, as I defend it here, becomes a belief which is in practice irrefutable at the cost of becoming a belief that is in practice vacuous. Where the criteria for the truth of a position are laid down, so to speak, from within that position, then it does appear, at least in the present case, that the word 'truth' is being misused, for it becomes impossible to differentiate a position for which one claims truth (in the ordinary sense) and a position which one merely entertains because of its aesthetic power. Traditional Christianity is, of course, not vacuous and does claim in unambiguous terms to be true. The philosophy of religion of my essay is thus in yet another respect inconsistent with the faith it tried to elucidate.

This is not to say that I regard my essay as therefore rendered devoid of all interest. It is extremely important that the position I held then should be fully worked out and its consequences properly understood. But I regard the working out as having resulted in a quite unintended *reductio ad absurdum*. 'The man who speaks like this is beyond argument,' I concluded; and again: 'Belief cannot argue with unbelief; it can only preach to it.' I now believe that this is indeed the outcome of this position; but I now also regard its irrationalism as both false and dangerous. And I am in the debt of those critics such as Basil Mitchell and Antony Flew, who combined from different positions to make this clear to me.

One final point of a very different kind: this book was one of the first to appear in the Library of Philosophy and Theology, published in Great Britain by SCM Press, which was then edited by Ronald Gregor Smith and myself. When Ronald Gregor Smith died so untimely a death last year (and *his* death would have been untimely whenever it happened), the loss was to all the subjects with which this book is concerned. He cared about philosophy and science as well as about his own subject of theology. He was a poet. He loved the thought of David Hume as well as that of Martin Buber. We shall never cease to be in his debt.

November 1969   *Alasdair MacIntyre*

I
CONTEMPORARY
SCIENTIFIC MYTHOLOGY

STEPHEN TOULMIN

I

SCIENTIFIC THEORIES AND
SCIENTIFIC MYTHS

IF we go into an eighteenth-century library, we may be
surprised at the number of theological works it contains.
Baxter's *Reasons*, Ogden's *Articles*, Warburton's *Divine
Legation*: there they stand, and with them the sermons, row
on row of them, solid, calf-bound, imposing; yet somehow
(we feel) period pieces, as foreign to us in our day as the wigs
and top-boots in a Hogarth print. For a member of Dr
Johnson's Literary Club, it was as important to be *au fait* with
Ogden or Warburton as it was to be ready with an apt quota-
tion from Pope or Horace. Anyone who has read his Boswell
knows how often, when gossip was exhausted, conversation in
Johnson's circle turned to ethics, philosophy or theology; for
these were subjects in which any educated man felt an
obligation to be interested.

We in the twentieth century, however, feel different
obligations. It is science we like to be up-to-date in, Freud
and Hoyle we choose to know about. We are interested less
in the doctrine of the First Cause than in physical cosmology,
while the Ten Commandments and the nature of the moral
sense seem tepid to us when set alongside the theory of the
super-ego. *Autres temps autres mœurs*: the emphasis in polite
conversation has shifted. If we are puzzled by the shelves of
collected sermons in our ancestors' libraries, that is because
we forget how far scientific and aesthetic questions have
replaced moral and theological ones as the staple of dinner-
table-talk; and how far the popular scientist has won over the
audience of the popular preacher.

At first sight, this appears a remarkable change, and

3

certainly, so far as prestige is concerned, science has made great advances at the expense of philosophy and theology: that much is a commonplace. But is the change as great as it seems? Are people really no longer interested in all those serious topics which preoccupied their ancestors, finding themselves absorbed instead in some quite different set of problems? Or are the same old cargoes being carried (so to speak) in fresh bottoms, under a new flag? What answer we give to that question depends on this: how far the problems the man-in-the-street expects the scientist to solve for him are ones about which a scientist is specially qualified to speak. So before we are too impressed by the change it is worth asking whether, when we turn to works of popular science, the questions we are interested in are always genuinely scientific ones. I think this is only partly so, and in what follows I shall try to show why. Often enough, we tend to ask too much of science, and to read into the things the scientist tells us implications that are not there—which in the nature of the case cannot be there; drawing from scraps of information about, for instance, physics, conclusions which no amount of physics could by itself establish. Sometimes our questions are clearly the same as those that the eighteenth-century theologians tackled: a discussion about free-will is none the less about free-will for bringing in Heisenberg's 'uncertainty relation'. But more often we are unaware of what we are doing, and turn to the scientist as to an expert, an authority, even when he is entitled to no more than a private opinion.

Quite a lot of popular science books encourage us in this, and present these opinions as the latest results of scientific research. Their authors do not confine themselves to explaining some scientific investigation, some novel theory or discovery about phenomena which had previously not been understood. They go on to do something more, something different, something which can hardly be called science at all. As a result there has grown up a sort of scientific harlequinade in the shape of an independent body of ideas which play a considerable part in the layman's picture of science, but in science proper none at all. The Running-Down Universe,

Evolution with a capital E: these are two examples which (I shall try to show) are not so much scientific discoveries as scientific myths.

'Scientific Myths': the very phrase is apt to sound a little paradoxical. For we like to think of myths as a thing of the past. We pride ourselves that they have been killed, and killed, furthermore, by science. Atlas, Ceres, Wotan, Poseidon . . . *nous n'avons pas besoin de ces hypothèses.* These names are for us the last relics of an outmoded system of thought, which attempted to explain in one way—by personification—things which we can now explain much better in another. The stability of the earth, the fertility of the soil, the ever-varying behaviour of the sea, these are all things we understand well enough nowadays without the need to bring in giants and goddesses.

This view of myths is, however, a shallow one. The attempt to explain natural phenomena by personification may be dead, or moribund. But many of the motives which produced the myths of the Greek and Northern peoples remain active in us still. In consequence it is not enough to regard the old stories only as half-baked science. They were that, no doubt, among other things. When people used to talk about Zeus or Wotan as the thunder-maker, they certainly thought that in these terms the occurrence of thunderstorms could be explained, so to this extent the notion of Zeus played for them the part which the notion of atmospheric electricity does for us. Variations in natural phenomena, failure of the harvest or turbulence of the sea, were likewise to be understood in anthropomorphic terms, as the moods of divine agents, Ceres or Poseidon. But there was always something more to these myths. Zeus was not only the thunder-maker, he was also the Father of Men; and as such he played a very different role. For mere disinterested curiosity over unexplained phenomena would never have led people to talk of a 'divine father', whether in Heaven or on Olympus: that has never been a purely scientific conception. So, though with the progress of science the motions of the sea and the stars and the growth of the corn have ceased to be for us the work of hidden hands,

5

nevertheless some of the motives for myth-making are with us to-day as much as ever they were. Myths are with us, too. Our difficulty is, to know in which direction to look for the myths of the twentieth century, to recognize and unravel the non-scientific motives behind them, and to see these motives at work.

If we do think ourselves myth-free, when we are not, that is (I am suggesting) largely because the material from which we construct our myths is taken from the sciences themselves. The situation is the one we meet in those trickiest of crime stories, in which the detective himself turns out to have done the deed: he is the last man we suspect. There are of course other reasons too why we find it hard to recognize our own myths. To begin with, they are hard to spot, as our own fallacies are hard to spot, just because they are our own: fallacies, we are tempted to think, are the faults in *other* people's arguments, and myths the queer ideas people *used* to have about the universe. Again, we are inclined to suppose that myths must necessarily be anthropomorphic, and that personification is the unique road to myth. But this assumption is baseless: the myths of the twentieth century, as we shall see, are not so much anthropomorphic as mechanomorphic. And why, after all, should not the purposes of myth be served as effectively by picturing the world in terms of mythical machines as by invoking mythical personages? Still, in the main, it is because our contemporary myths are scientific ones that we fail to acknowledge them as being myths at all. The old picture of the world has been swept away; Poseidon and Wotan have suffered death by ridicule; and people not unnaturally look to the scientist for a substitute.

Therein lies the misunderstanding, for only in part were the ancient myths half-baked science, and only in part was their role an explanatory one. So far as this was so, we can reasonably look on the natural sciences as their descendants; but only so far. The other non-scientific motives behind them remain, and the sciences are not obliged to cater for these. The notion of atmospheric electricity, for example, was introduced to account in a scientific way for lightning and thunder, and to that extent displaced Zeus as the thunder-maker, but it was never intended to take over Zeus' role as the 'divine father' as well. Rather, the two roles have been separated, so that thunderstorms are no longer regarded in the old way, as a topic for theology.

It is not enough, however, to suspect that there may be such 'scientific myths' : we must also know how to recognize them when we come across them. How are we to do this? Partly, I have argued, by seeing what sorts of question they are used to answer : if a conception, however scientific its birth or ancestry, is used in practice only as a way of dealing with non-scientific questions—whether ethical, philosophical or theological—then it is no longer following the trade of its forefathers, and has ceased itself to be a scientific term at all. Again, there are some terms of irreproachably scientific origin which begin after a time to live double lives: as well as their primary, scientific *métier* they acquire part-time jobs of another kind. If we find evidence of such duplicity, our suspicions will be confirmed.

This is a clue, but it is one which immediately raises further questions. How is it, for instance, that such a double life is possible? Scientists take so much care in defining their terms that serious ambiguities cannot, surely, remain : if the meaning of their terms were not clear, one would expect this to have its effect on their work—to lead, that is, to trouble within science itself. And in any case, if a scientist has been true to his declared method, and has introduced into his theories only those terms which he absolutely requires in order to explain the phenomena he has been studying, what room is there for equivocation?

The answer to this question is a double one, partly historical, partly logical. The ideal of a science which contains nothing but what is forced on us by the phenomena we are studying is only an ideal : it is not, and never will be, an accomplished fact. As a matter of method, no doubt, scientists do develop and modify their theories and conceptions in just such ways as will (so far as they can see) best accommodate the phenomena; nor are they prepared to allow outside considerations to obstruct such developments as the phenomena require. But the theories they subscribe to as a result, whether in the sixth century B.C. or in the fifteenth or twentieth A.D., fall short of the purist's ideal for two reasons. To begin with, their historical origins are against them. Anyone can see the points of resemblance between the cosmology of Plato's *Timaeus* and the Near Eastern myths which it was intended to displace; and, though many of these residual elements of myth have since dropped out of our science, it is imprudent to point the finger of scorn at Plato (as Sarton does) until we have inquired whether this elimination has been completed. It is wiser to recognize that, as our scientific ideas develop, there will always be a tug-of-war between tradition and method: a scientist's *methods* may be completely empirical, yet his investigations will have no direction without the guidance of a pre-existing body of ideas, some of which may turn out under scrutiny to be survivals from surprisingly far back.

This factor may, as the centuries pass, be of less and less importance, but the other is of permanent relevance. However much the sciences may eventually outgrow their historical swaddling-bands, there must always be something more to the framework of ideas which constitutes a theory than the bare recapitulation of the phenomena it is used to explain. The structure of a scientific theory may be built up entirely from the bricks of observation, but the exact position the bricks occupy depends on the layout of the scientist's conceptual scaffolding; and this element of scaffolding, which the scientist introduces himself, is always open to misinterpretation.

Neither of these factors is one which need affect the scientific value and validity of a theory. If a term like 'evolution' comes to be used ambiguously—having both a pure biological use and an extended, philosophical or mythological use—this ambiguity is not one which will necessarily show up in a strictly biological argument. The aspects of the notion which are put to mythological use may not be ones that bear either way on any biological questions; and so long as they do not do so, the notion will preserve all its power within biology.

8

Even to speak of ambiguity in this context may therefore be too strong. What we have rather is a choice between two interpretations of a term, a narrow one and a wide one: a narrow one, whose use and justification lie wholly within the natural sciences, and a wider, extended one, whose justification and use both lie in part elsewhere.

With this point in mind, we can clear out of the way one elementary misunderstanding. When I go on to argue that some familiar notion—The Running-Down Universe, for instance, or Evolution regarded as 'the Cosmic Process'—is a scientific myth, I shall not be making a point which raises questions of a straight-forward scientific kind. In particular, I shall not be casting any shadow of doubt either on the laws of thermodynamics, or on the doctrine that species have developed by variation and natural selection. There are, no doubt, plenty of people who still reject Darwin's theory even as biology. I am not one of them: in its essentials it seems to me among the finest and most firmly established products of biological thought. The claim that Evolution is sometimes treated as a myth must not, then, be misunderstood: it is quite distinct from any possible claim that, as a scientific theory, there is something dubious or unsound or even speculative about the Darwinian view of the origin of species.

People do, it is true, sometimes say 'So-and-So is a myth', meaning only that the belief is untrue or unsound; and this might be said of Darwin's theory by an anti-evolutionist, as a contemptuous way of dismissing it. But do not let us fall victims to this sort of loose expression. To use the word myth only as a term of abuse is to rob ourselves of a useful distinction. Not all out-dated scientific concepts were myths, nor vice versa—caloric, for instance, had no mythological significance. So, if we talk about scientific myths, let us do so strictly; in order to raise not scientific issues but logical ones. Granted that the theory of evolution or the laws of thermodynamics are all that a scientist can ask; granted that their position within biology and physics is as firmly established as it could be; if this may be allowed, just how much is accomplished? What sorts of conclusions are forced on us by our acceptance of these theories, and on which do they have no direct bearing? These are the questions we must ask. If we find that the theories are regularly invoked in support of conclusions of a kind to which, as scientific theories, they have no relevance; further, if these conclusions are of a sort with which mythologies have from the earliest times been concerned; then we can say with some justice, not that the theories themselves are 'only myths', but rather that on these occasions their conceptions are being inflated into Scientific Myths.

Once again, then, how are we to recognize when a scientific term is being pressed into service of a non-scientific kind? The chief point to look out for is the following. When a technical term is introduced into a science, or an everyday word like force or energy is given a fresh, scientific application, it has a clearly defined place in a theory—a theory whose task it is to explain some limited range of phenomena. What gives the term a meaning for science is the part it plays in these explanations. One can think of such a term as a piece in a jig-saw puzzle; and, like such a piece, it loses most of its significance as soon as we try to make anything of it out of context. We can take the notion of universal gravitation (gravity, for short) as an example. When Newton introduced this idea, his purpose was a limited and tangible one: namely, to account for the motions of the planets, the comets and the moon in terms of the same laws of motion as held for terrestrial bodies. And when one says 'account for', this means (as he himself took care to emphasize)[1] account in a mathematical way. For Newton's purposes, the term 'gravity' acquired its meaning with the introduction of the inverse-square law; and this in its turn earned a place in physical theory because it could be used to work out how, in this or that situation, celestial or terrestrial bodies can be expected to move. As a piece of planetary dynamics, Newton's theory needed no other justification. He saw that in due course the theory might be amplified to deal with other phenomena, and the mode of action of gravity might thereby be discovered; but, he insisted, we must not

[1] Cf.: Newton, *Mathematical Principles of Natural Philosophy*, ed. F. Cajori (1934), pp. 550–1: 'The System of the World', §2.

jump to conclusions; and in any case his notion of 'gravity' should not be taken as having any implications outside dynamical theory.

It is to some such modest but solid job that all scientific terms are put, 'evolution', 'entropy' and so on, quite as much as 'gravity', and it is vital for the progress of science that their meaning should be limited in this way. It is just because the terms of the sciences are so well defined, and defined in a way which is closely tied down to the phenomena, that questions in science can be settled: only because this is so can scientists hope to answer definitely the questions that arise for them, by looking to see whether things actually happen in nature in the manner the theory suggests—in this way, they can usually come to agree upon one answer and reject the alternatives.

If this is forgotten, difficulties are created. Suppose we extend a carefully defined scientific term beyond the range of its theory, and use it in more ambitious but less tangible speculations, then there will be snags at once. For whereas before this was done one could check the soundness of one's speculations against the facts, now things will be different: there will be no way of checking what is said by experiment or observation, and so, scientifically speaking, nothing to choose between one possible answer and another. And if this is so, if when a dispute arises there are now no conceivable observations to be made by which we can decide between the disputants, then there can be no question of either side in the dispute claiming for his doctrine the support of the theory concerned. The theory will be neutral between all such views.

Newton realized this also. It was not that he had any objection to wider speculations: as we know now, he spent a surprisingly large part of his time on natural theology, the interpretation of biblical prophecies and other non-scientific problems. But in these speculations he did not keep appealing to 'gravity'. The term had a clear meaning in dynamics, and it could play a part in theology only if it were given a radically different sense. When he came to expound his theory of gravitation, therefore, he put aside all wider questions, and the only rival views he bothered to consider were other genuinely physical ones—for instance, those of Descartes and his followers.

In Descartes's picture of the solar system one must think of the sun as surrounded by a vortex, and of the planets as carried round about it like floating chips: the idea of gravitational attraction played no part in the account at all. To this theory, Newton's reply was simple. It is not enough, he argued, for a theory to provide a vivid picture of the solar system: one must work out the mathematical consequences of the view in detail. If this is done for the vortex theory, you cannot, short of the most implausible and groundless assumptions, make it fit the facts. In the first place, to talk of a vortex at all suggests that the space between the planets is filled with some kind of celestial bath-water, whose motions carry the planets round with it. But there is no independent evidence at all for supposing the existence of this fluid: indeed there are several reasons for rejecting the supposition—such as the fact that comets travel right across the solar system without showing any sign either of resistance from the fluid or of the effects of the vortex on their line of travel, and the fact that the satellites of each planet, however far it is from the sun, travel round it in the same manner. Further, to make the vortex theory work quantitatively, one must assume not merely the existence of this wholly impalpable fluid: one must imagine it endowed with physical properties (already, alas, indetectable) which vary greatly from point to point in space. A theory expressed in such terms as these could be of little use to science. Newton's own theory, by contrast, would account for all the observed motions of the comets, the planets and their satellites exactly, and without such a mass of arbitrary assumptions.[2]

No wonder Newton felt entitled to be satisfied with his theory. Yet it was assailed at once, from several directions. The followers of Descartes, of course, objected to the theory as physics; but others found wider reasons for attacking it. Leibniz, for instance, accused the doctrine of universal gravitation of being repugnant to common sense: to speak of the

[2] Cf.: *op. cit.*, pp. 385–96: Bk. II, sect. ix.

heavenly bodies as gravitating towards one another was, he said, 'a strange fiction'.[3] He further agreed with Berkeley in finding the implications of Newton's views impious, if not actually atheistical, for reasons which we do not now find it easy to accept.

These wider criticisms distressed Newton, but he did not spend much time answering them. Of course what he spoke of as gravity was an extension of the everyday, terrestrial notion, and must be understood as such. Leibniz might want to stand by the old sense of the term—the one enshrined in seventeenth-century 'common sense'; but if one looked at the uses to which Newton put his extended notion, one would see how the extension could be justified.

Before his time, the notion of gravity had an application only to bodies on the earth—pick up a chair and it feels heavy (*gravis*), let it go and it falls (gravitates) to the ground. The heavenly bodies, by contrast, were quite unlike chairs. They moved in their stable orbits round the sun or kept their places in the more distant firmament—the notion of gravitation manifestly had no relevance to their behaviour. The hypothesis that the planets were *massive* was no doubt an intelligible one; that they were *heavy* would have been a less intelligible suggestion; and to talk of heavenly bodies falling or gravitating would have called to mind only the falling stars which appeared in spring and autumn to drop through the night sky, or the thunderbolts which from time to time would strike the earth and awe the superstitious.

Newton's theory changed all that. The regular motion of the planets round the sun, which his predecessors had so carefully described—this too, he declared, was an effect of 'gravity' and a case of 'gravitation', just as much as the weight of a chair or its fall to the ground when released. The view might seem paradoxical to some: the stars and planets have no visible means of support, yet they do not, like terrestrial bodies, fall to the ground for lack of it. But the view has a point, and a *scientific* point at that. One can represent the motions of the planets round the sun with a degree of

[3] Leibniz-Clarke correspondence: Leibniz's fifth letter, §35.

accuracy exceeding anything detectable by observation in Newton's time by regarding them as freely moving bodies, acted on only by his 'inverse square force': exactly the same force can be appealed to in explanation of those terrestrial phenomena which alone had hitherto been called gravitational. This was all that was in question in calling the motion of the planets 'gravitational', or an effect of 'gravity'.

As for the question, whether the new theory was atheistical or not, even to ask this was to read things into the theory. What Newton had been doing was a piece of physics, as a result of which he had been able to explain in a mathematical way how the planets moved. The solar system, could, he thought, be none the less wonderful—none the less a tribute to the foresight of the Almighty—for our having gone thus far towards understanding it. Indeed he himself was inclined to think the opposite. To have shown that one set of mathematical principles underlay so many varied dynamical phenomena should (as he put it) 'work with considering men for the belief of a Deity', so he could see nothing impious in the theory.[4] In any case, when it came to natural theology, what told in the balance was not the details of the theory. The precise form of his law of gravity could not therefore be relevant to any theological issue: the success of an inverse-cube law would have been no less impressive than that of his own theory. All that was at issue, for theology, was the rationality of the universe, and this was something which any successful and comprehensive theory helped to vindicate. Meanwhile, there was plenty within physics to keep him busy—plenty of genuinely scientific questions, which one could hope to answer by reference to the telescope or an experiment. He had no time or inclination to defend the notion of gravitation from other people's misinterpretations.

From this example we can perhaps see what is liable to happen when scientific terms are used, not to explain anything, but for other purposes—for instance, as the raw material of myths. Technical scientific notions taken by

[4] Cf. his letters to Richard Bentley, and the General Scholium added to the third edition of the *Mathematical Principles*, pp. 543–7.

themselves have, as we saw, about as much meaning as isolated pieces taken out of a jig-saw puzzle. If we try to do other things with them—for example, to build a comprehensive 'world-view' of a philosophical kind from them—we are forgetting this fact, and treating them as though they were pieces of a single, cosmic jig-saw. This has two unfortunate consequences. First, you cannot get pieces taken from different puzzles to fit together at all except by distorting them; and in the second place, if one man forces them together in one way and one in another, nobody will be able to say that one or the other of the pictures so produced is, scientifically speaking, the 'right' one.

These difficulties arise again when physical or biological theories are appealed to in an attempt to solve problems in, for instance, ethics or political theory. To begin with, all the scientific terms used get distorted in the process, and no longer keep the clear meaning they have in science proper: this fact alone shows the gulf between scientific myths and the theories whose concepts they exploit. Furthermore, when two people appeal to the same scientific theory as backing for different 'world-views' or different political doctrines, how can we even set about choosing between them? Within science, we can at any rate prove our views in practice. But when we put scientific terms to non-scientific uses, this, the chief merit of a scientific approach, is lost. For all that experiment or observation can show, one scientific myth is as good as another.

II

THE LIMITS OF COSMOLOGY

MEN have always been curious to know about the Beginning of All Things and the End of All Things, so mythologies have at all times contained Creation stories, and often Apocalypses too. We are beginning to realize now what complex things these myths are: how many strands of thought are entangled together in them, and how mistaken it is to suppose that they represent only attempts to say what happened a very, very long time ago and more, and what is going eventually, eventually to happen. But that they have represented these among other things is past question, and it is worth unravelling this strand from the others and looking at it by itself. So let us take the questions 'What happened before anything else happened?' and 'What is going to happen after everything else has happened?' and see what we can make of them.

We certainly cannot expect these questions to be easy to answer. If scientists have any contribution to make to their answering, we must presumably expect it to be a tentative one, for how could it be anything else? If the questions are meant as historical ones, they must be tackled as such; and there are certain difficulties about any sort of historical study, whether it is the diplomatic history of Europe during the last quarter-century, the archaeological reconstruction of a civilization dead for three millennia, the geological story of the formation of the coal-measures, or the astronomical history of the solar system. In each case we must expect the more remote past to be shrouded in greater mystery than the less, and we cannot hope, short of great good fortune, to reach the same certainty about the remoter past that we can about the more recent.

Strokes of luck do occur sometimes, such as the preservation in peat of the lake-village at Glastonbury, thanks to which we know a good deal about life there during the last centuries B.C., though the early centuries A.D. are still in darkness. But by and large one can fairly say that the further back we go the less we can hope to find out. What goes for the reconstruction of the past holds with greater force, if that be possible, for the prediction of the future. The longer the term of the predictions we make, the more qualified they must be, and the same darkness that envelops the remoter past falls even more quickly when we look into the more distant future.

This at any rate must be true of any attempt to argue methodically from evidence about the state of things to-day to conclusions about the state of things a long, long time ago or far, far into the future. We do not find, and perhaps we do not expect to find, the same modesty about Creation Myths. It may be that, intellectually, the Book of Genesis is the worse for lacking these qualifications: this I am not going to discuss. What is clear, however, is that a scientific account of these things must certainly not lack them: '. . . And the Earth, so far as we can ascertain, was void; and the evidence tends on the whole to support the view that darkness was upon the face of the deep . . .': this may seem pedestrian, but it is the business of scientists to be pedestrian, to keep one foot on the ground of their evidence, and not to run, leap or vault off into unsupportable speculations.

With these cautions in mind, I want to turn and look at the things scientists have recently had to say about the remotest past, and about the remotest future. The cautions are necessary, for in each case one finds their utterances strangely confident and un-tentative. If things had worked out as we should have expected, nothing in science would have been less certain than our speculations about the very beginning of all things, and about their ultimate fate. Yet when scientists turn to discuss these topics, a sudden fluency descends upon them, as though the mist through which the past and future are seen was, when we reach the extreme limits, suddenly lifted, and a clear vision of the first and last events

granted to us. What has happened? Is it that, like the archae-
ologists of Glastonbury, students of physical cosmology have
been blessed with unexpected good fortune, in the shape of
striking and conclusive evidence in a field where they could
hope for no more than ambiguous scraps? Or has their confidence a different source—is their determination to get at
answers to these questions affecting their sense of relevance,
and leading them to find evidence where there is none?
Here is a question at any rate worth posing.

Let us start with the stories about the uttermost future: in
particular, with a doctrine which is a common-place of
popular scientific addresses, the doctrine of the 'running-down
universe'. This is something which hardly needs expounding
in detail: most of us must have come across one or another of
the apocalyptic utterances in which physicists, philosophers
and theologians discuss the ultimate 'death by freezing' of the
entire universe. The central suggestion, it will be remembered,
is this: that one of the best-established laws of physics, the
one called The Second Law of Thermodynamics, obliges us
to think of the universe as a one-way system bound of necessity
to become uninhabitable, that—saving some sort of divine
intervention—all activity in the universe is as certain to peter
out as a clock which no one winds is bound to stop. Though
the exact date at which life as we know it will be extinguished
may be a matter of doubt; though the time involved may be
measured in millions of millennia; nevertheless, when the
temperature drops far enough, the end must come, and life
will be over for good. The running-down of the universe may
be slow, but it is (we are told) inexorable. Whatever else may
be uncertain about the future, that at any rate is in store . . .
and after that, nothing. This much we know for sure; and
all that there is left to us to do is to face the consequences of the
discovery.

This conclusion has always seemed a bit of a nightmare, and
just how we should compose ourselves in the face of it people
have not been able to agree. Philosophers like Russell and
Ramsey, theologians—Dean Inge being an example—scientists such as Ostwald, a Nobel Prize chemist: writers of all

kinds have concerned themselves with its implications.[1] Recently, too, Fred Hoyle has even argued that, as a matter of physics, the Second Law may not be universally applicable after all, that processes may be going on in the universe which are capable of making up for the Universal Unwinding and putting fresh power into the Spring, so that we can breathe freely again. But for once let us leave the details of what they all say, both the physics and the attitudinizing, and see whether we cannot get behind the dispute, asking: Was there ever any real cause for a nightmare? Whatever the scientific rights and wrongs of Hoyle's new theory, need we ever have felt worried in the first place? Could any discovery physicists might make ever in fact compel us to regard the universe-as-a-whole as a 'running-down clock'?

There is no denying that, if we are in fact forced to accept this picture of the universe, if physicists can really predict the eventual extinction of all effective temperature-differences, and if this prediction is as utterly and absolutely inescapable as we have been told, then—even though the moment of doom may be millions of millennia away—this must make a considerable difference to our view of the world. There are, no doubt, several possible reactions. One can be heroic about it, like ocean voyagers who continue to dress for dinner even though they have discovered that the ship is sinking under them, feeling that there is a certain dignity in putting on a good show in the meantime. One can be Epicurean, like Frank Ramsey, who called for a sense of perspective: 'In time the world will cool', he wrote, 'and everything will die, but that is a long time off still, and its present value at compound discount is almost nothing'. Or again, one can be other-worldly: if the scientists now confirm the view that the world of space and time is a leaky vessel, that (one can argue) shows all the more that we should pin our hopes Elsewhere. But whichever our reaction may be, whether we choose Jeremiah, Epicurus or Casabianca as our model, we must do something to reconcile ourselves to the inevitable future. As Ostwald

[1] F. P. Ramsey, *The Foundations of Mathematics*, p. 291; W. R. Inge, *God and the Astronomers*; F. W. Ostwald, *Die Philosophie der Werte*, p. 98.

put it: 'We must in all circumstances learn to accept the fact that at some indefinite but far-off time our civilization is doomed to go under . . . and that, in the longest run, the sum of all human endeavour has no recognizable significance.'

But all this is conditional. And the conditional clauses are these: *if* the picture of the universe as a running-down clock really has all the authority and backing that it seems to; *if* it rests on a proper reading of the Second Law of Thermodynamics; *if*, when we are told that it is theoretically impossible to decrease the entropy of an isolated system, this impossibility is of a kind that calls for regret or resignation or fatalism. These will turn out to be three very sizeable 'ifs'.

At this point, now the word 'entropy' has appeared and needs explaining, an excursion in the direction of physics is unavoidable. I have also quoted the standard formulation of the Second Law of Thermodynamics—namely, that in a thermally isolated system all physical changes take place in such a way that the entropy remains constant or increases— and it is necessary to see what this law implies in a practical case. These two explanations are best given together. So, by comparison with our earlier example, we may perhaps say this: as the term 'gravity' is introduced for purposes of mechanics, so the term 'entropy' is introduced for purposes of thermodynamics, that is, the theory of heat-exchanges. Where the law of gravitation is used in the first place in explaining, in a mathematical way, how the planets, the comets, falling bodies and the waters of the oceans may be expected to move, the Second Law of Thermodynamics is used in the first place in working out what efficiency you can expect to get from a steam-engine operating at a given temperature, how much power will be needed to run a refrigerator under given conditions, and so on.

'In the first place', we have to say, as the law soon acquires extensive affiliations of a more abstract and theoretical kind. These we can look at later: it will be as well to start by considering the law in its simpler, 'phenomenological' form, in which its cash-value in terms of actual happenings is more easily grasped. In practical terms, then, the force of the law is, that if a system of bodies is shielded from exchanges of heat with surrounding bodies—completely lagged, that is—the temperatures of the various bodies in the system will tend to even out, the hotter ones cooling and the colder ones warming up. Just as we have the technical word 'temperature' as the numerical counterpart of the familiar words 'hot' and 'cold', so we have the technical word 'entropy' as the numerical measure of the degree to which this evening-out process has gone on. The exact manner in which entropy is measured we need not enter into. What we do need to notice is that, at the phenomenological level, the law has to be stated in terms of 'thermally isolated' systems. If we are to know how far the law is applicable to any chosen system in nature, we must first inquire how far it is shielded from thermal interaction with its surroundings; roughly speaking, how far it is lagged.

How are we to draw from a law of this kind any conclusions about the universe as a whole? Can we do so, indeed? From the start we saw grounds for suspicion. How physicists feel so sure about what is going to happen all those millions of years away must be a bit of a mystery. If, like the astronomers in H. G. Wells's story *In the Days of the Comet*, they had the best of evidence that another vast heavenly body was about to collide with the earth, things would be rather different. That discovery would be something like a 'death-sentence': we should have some reason then to start saying our prayers. So the first thing which was fishy about the 'running-down universe' argument was the indirectness of the experimental evidence. If an astronomer were to warn us of the imminent impact of a comet, we could at least ask him for direct evidence, such as the observed trajectory of the comet over the past weeks and days. If the ultimate fate of the universe were predicted on the basis of this sort of argument, we must therefore ask: what sort of evidence is relied on? In the first place, observations on the performance of steam-engines. . . . To which the layman might be tempted to reply, 'Quite: and the Roman augurs used to predict the fall of cities from a study of the intestines of birds.'

In fact, this comparison is far from just; and besides, the

crucial objections to the argument lie elsewhere. It is by a more complex train of reasoning that the ultimate freeze-up is predicted, so that it is not enough to complain about the indirectness of the evidence. In any case that is not the target on which we should concentrate our fire, for, so long as we feel only that the evidence is at fault—so long as the clock picture itself is left uncriticized—it will be natural to suppose that, given time to collect more evidence, physicists may yet succeed in establishing the doctrine. At any rate, the idea will not seem absurd.

This, however, is what really needs examining: whether physics in general or thermodynamics in particular can have this sort of implication at all. To ask this question is not to cast doubt on the acceptability of the Second Law as a law of thermodynamics. (This, to repeat, I am regarding as un-questioned.) It is to ask rather, as a logical matter, whether to appeal to the law in support of metaphysical doctrines in the sphere of eschatology is not to misapply it.

Perhaps putting the issue in this way begs the question, by implying that the doctrines we are concerned with are not physical but metaphysical ones. This certainly needs to be established, since a great deal turns on just this fact. So I want to argue that the thesis which likens the universe to a running-down clock is a double one, one half genuine physics, the other half metaphysical, and to show what is involved in assuming that both halves can be established by the same scientific methods.

We are told (it must be noted) not only that our earth will eventually cool down to an unendurable extent, and all life be extinguished, but also that this is only one aspect of the inexorable decay of the whole universe. If the first half of the thesis alone were advanced, the issue would indeed be largely one of physics. We can certainly visualize life on the earth coming to an end if all the regions at present inhabitable were to freeze up, and, if this were all that was claimed, we should be faced with a straightforward prediction. Still, it is a prediction which could be made with confidence only on the most unlikely assumptions. After all that men have managed to achieve during the last few hundred years, are they going to sit by and let themselves be gradually snuffed out, over a period of millions and millions of years? It needs little enough imagination to suppose their finding ways of keeping up the surface temperature of the earth, developing in their descend- ants greater resistance to cold, if need be jet-propelling the orbit of the planet a little nearer the sun. There are countless things they might do to falsify the prediction, many of them at the moment no more than Science Fiction, but none of them out of the question if you consider the amount of time at their disposal. As a practical threat to the future of the human race, the cooling of the earth cannot rate very high; we can all of us name several far more serious.

This reply, however, deals only with the first half of the thesis, and if we stopped at that point we might be accused of missing the real significance of the Second Law. 'Any things which men did in this way', it might be said, 'would be merely palliatives, and could only postpone the end. It is not as an immediate, practical obstacle that the effects of the Second Law are important: their true significance becomes apparent only when you widen your vision to embrace the whole universe, and when you realize that to counter the action of the law is more than a practical problem—it is a theoretical impossibility.' 'The second law of thermodynamics states' (and now I am quoting Sir Harold Spencer-Jones, the last Astronomer-Royal) 'that entropy in the universe must always increase; so that all change will eventually cease, and this ending will come in a finite time—the universe is running down and must eventually come to a stop—and this law, so far as we can tell, holds a supreme position amongst the laws of nature.'[2]

Here the second half of the thesis begins to come into play, and the nightmare impression of fatalism begins. So long as we thought only of the earth the problem seemed of manage- able size, and so long as it was a practical problem we were tackling there seemed hope of finding practical means of getting round it. But the problem cannot be got around, it is

[2] *Science News*, No. 32 (Penguin Books 1954), p. 24.

now argued, as what we are up against is a theoretical, not a practical barrier; and further it is not the solar system alone but the whole universe which is grinding to a stop, so that all our palliatives will in the long run be in vain. However, it is at this point also (so far as I can see) that the issue ceases to be a genuinely physical one. Suppose it is completely established that the Second Law can be applied to all physical systems thermally isolated from the rest of the universe, does it necessarily apply also to the universe taken as a whole? And does the fact that the impossibility it tells us of is a theoretical rather than a practical one imply that it is exceedingly, indeed infinitely, difficult to overcome?

These are the propositions we must question, for two reasons: both because their soundness is regularly taken for granted when this subject is under discussion, and because it is only by introducing them into the argument that the clock picture can be established—without them, the fatalist *Weltanschauung* shrinks into a far-distant challenge to the technology of our descendants. We can concede that the Second Law has won for itself a supreme position in the structure of physical theory, and that it is now accepted as a 'universal law' which expresses a 'theoretical impossibility': what we must examine is the further inference that the law tells us something ineluctable about the universe-as-a-whole. So let us look at the two phrases 'a universal law' and 'theoretically impossible', and see what traps they hold in store for us if we are not on our guard.

First, then, the phrase 'a universal law'. To say that the Second Law of Thermodynamics is a universal law is to say that it holds *universally*, in the same way as the law of gravitation. (Of course, since Fred Hoyle put forward his theory we are not so sure that it does in fact hold universally after all, but this is by the way: for our purposes it is better to suppose that the universality of the law is established and ask what follows from that.) A universal law, in other words, is one which has been found applicable not just to some but to all systems of physical objects which satisfy the conditions laid down in the theory. The law of gravitation is universal if and only if it holds for all pairs of objects having mass; and the Second Law of Thermodynamics is universal if and only if it holds for any thermally isolated system, whatever and wherever it may be—and holds the more nearly for any system we choose, the more completely this system is thermally isolated from its surroundings. By itself, the fact that a law is a universal one implies nothing about the universe-as-a-whole. The fact that the law of gravitational attraction held universally would never be taken as implying that 'the universe' must be attracting something, any more than the discovery that tooth-cleaning was a universal practice would imply that 'the universe' must clean its teeth. A statement which 'holds universally' is one thing, a statement about 'the universe' is another, and a step from one to the other will always require justification.

In the case of gravitation this step is never taken: in the case of entropy it is taken regularly, but the justification is assumed—indeed, from the way in which it is taken one would not guess that any question of justification arose. According to the late Astronomer-Royal, for instance, the Second Law 'states that entropy in the universe must always increase', and that is that. But this is a sheer mis-statement of the law. The Second Law by itself states nothing about 'the universe', any more than does the law of gravitation. The most it could do would be to *imply* something about the universe, and it could do that only if we also knew how far the universe was itself a thermally isolated system. Until this additional question has been squarely faced, we cannot be satisfied that there is any warrant in physics for the idea of the whole universe coming to a stop.

How could this further question be settled? Is it, in fact, the sort of question a physicist could ever hope to answer? One of two things seems to be needed: either scientists must make direct observations to establish the universe's degree of isolation, or they must find some way of proving from other established facts what the extent of its isolation is. But once we start to imagine possible experiments, and inquire what observations would really serve us here, we come up against grave difficulties. These are not the practical difficulties, of making observations on so vast an object of study. They are conceptual or (if you prefer) intellectual difficulties, to do with the sense of the question itself. For the question is, how far the universe-as-a-whole is a thermally isolated system, a 'thermally isolated' system being one which is shielded against all interchanges of heat with bodies outside itself; and what are we to make of the question, whether or no the universe-as-a-whole is shielded thermally from its surroundings? Since every material system and part of space there is forms (by definition) a part of the universe, we have left ourselves no room to talk about the universe's having surroundings. It is not just that outside the universe there is nothing, so that from that quarter it is incapable of drawing any fresh supply of heat: it makes no more sense to talk of the surroundings of the universe as empty than it does to talk of them as full, for in this context the distinction between 'inside' and 'outside' has no use. The prime difficulty lies deeper: it is that, whereas the question how far a given physical system is isolated from its surroundings has a clear enough meaning when asked about any bounded part of the universe—being equivalent to the question, to what extent heat exchanges are possible across the boundary—when asked about the universe-as-a-whole, its meaning is completely obscure.

It has long been notorious that questions which can be asked with perfect propriety of particular things, or parts of the world, or stretches of time tend to go wrong on us if we ask them about 'everything-there-is', or about 'the universe-as-a-whole', or about 'time itself'. This happens, for instance, with questions about 'the beginning of time', and it happens again in our present case. Talking about 'shielding the universe from its surroundings' has no more literal significance than talking about 'frying minus three eggs'. So unless some other more intelligible sense can be given to the question, the conditions necessary for us to apply the Second Law of Thermodynamics to the universe-as-a-whole are such as *cannot* be satisfied.

No alternative interpretation is normally offered, presumably because the need for it is not seen; and, though the hunt for suppressed premisses is always a speculative one, it is tempting to conclude that among them is an uncritical identification of 'universal laws' with 'laws of the universe'. Without this, the story that the universe is running down loses a good deal of its bite.

All this argument has, it is true, been presented in a form which applies to the Second Law in its simplest form—the one in which it applies most directly to the happenings in the world. Will the situation be altered if we treat the law differently, and consider it in some more abstract and theoretical form? 'Surely', it is said,[3] 'there are half a dozen alternative formulations of the law which do not mention "thermal isolation", and which can therefore be applied to the universe without assuming that it is "lagged" against something outside. If these formulations are equivalent to the original one, that shows that the clock-picture is valid after all.'

It would be a long and technical job to consider these alternative ways of stating the law one by one. In any case, two considerations may help us to see what the result would be. First, if the other formulations are truly equivalent to the original one or, being more general than it, reduce to it when one is considering thermal phenomena alone, then it is difficult to see how they can be in any different case when we come to apply them to 'the whole universe': if two questions are equivalent, a logical incongruity in one will be present in the other also. But secondly, the presence of the incongruity may be concealed, if the terms used are of an abstract and theoretical sort, for we may then fail to examine carefully enough the steps which must be taken if the law is to be used to account for actual physical phenomena.

This will be particularly liable to happen if the terms used are not obviously recondite, like 'entropy', but are borrowed from familiar speech and so apparently innocent. It may, for instance, be suggested that what the Second Law tells us is that 'order' is always lost in physical processes; and that to

[3] E.g. by Professor M. Polanyi in a comment on an earlier version of this essay (*Listener*, 15 Mar. 1951, p. 423).

say the universe is running down is to say that it is, so to speak, like a vast box full of packs of cards which, when shaken, lose their original order and become more and more mixed up.[4] But it is a long road from the theory of statistical mechanics, in which such analogies as this are at home, to the phenomena the theory is used to explain. How far the analogy between 'the whole universe' and a box full of cards can be pressed is something we cannot discover by theorizing alone, but only by considering in detailed, practical terms the relation between the theory and the facts it explains. For this purpose, the more abstract the formulation of a law we consider, the more confusing it will tend to be—especially if the terms in which it is expressed are deceptively concrete and familiar.

Appeals to abstract theory are, in any case, liable to cut both ways, as we can see if we turn to the second of the two notions that we set ourselves to examine. This was the notion of 'theoretical impossibility'. Seeing that this notion is what gives the clock-picture its air of fatalism, and is the source of the idea that the universal freeze-up is not just a threat, but an utterly inevitable doom, we had better take a closer look at it too.

When we read about 'theoretical impossibilities' in physics, we naturally think of them as things which are tremendously hard to do, and more. Lifting a ton weight single-handed—that is something no man yet born has been strong enough to do. But decreasing entropy, or cooling things below the Absolute Zero, or getting around Heisenberg's principle: these we understand to be harder still, still more obstinate—things in fact which there is utterly no hope of doing. To overcome a theoretical impossibility, we feel, we should have to surpass even the U.S. Transportation Corps, whose motto claims that they do the difficult every day, while 'the impossible takes a little longer'. Theoretical impossibilities seem not just harder than practical ones, but infinitely harder. This is one reason why the Second Law of Thermodynamics has made people feel fatalistic.

Yet is the difference between practical and theoretical

4 Cf. R. E. D. Clark, *Listener*, 15 Mar. 1951, p. 423.

impossibilities of this kind at all? There are strong grounds for thinking not, as may be seen if we look at a less technical example. Some things are, practically speaking, impossible to weigh; but, with others, weighing is theoretically impossible. We may find it hard to weigh a snowflake on a pair of kitchen scales, so hard as to be, practically speaking, impossible; but if someone says to us 'You can't weigh *fire*' the impossibility is more than a practical one—it is a theoretical one, which there is no question of our getting round by improving our instruments or increasing our ingenuity. This is not to say that weighing fire is that much harder again even than weighing a snowflake: it is to say something quite different. For what makes it impossible is not our want of ingenuity, or of suitable apparatus: no increase in skill or progress in instrument design could affect the issue. No: the root of the impossibility lies in the fact that our system of chemical classification or concepts does not admit 'fire' as a kind of substance.

Once this was not so. Only since the end of the eighteenth century has the distinction between chemical substances, physical processes and states of matter been clearly established. Before that, either 'fire' itself or phlogiston, the 'fiery element', was placed alongside water and air in the categories of science. Nowadays, however, the categories of chemistry are more refined. The process of combustion, the products of combustion, energy of the reaction, flaming gases and objects burned are all logically distinguishable; and the term *fire* has in consequence become the name of a process, not a substance. As a result, though questions about the weight of fire once had some sense, even if an obscure one, now they have none. Now we can no longer 'weigh fire', any more than we can 'weigh compassion' or 'weigh Tuesday'. Anything which it makes sense to talk of our weighing we may hope some day to weigh—including such things as the burning gases in a flame. Only if we chose to use the phrase 'weighing fire' to mean, say, weighing flames could the question of its possibility be revived.

This example may seem to turn on a matter of words—though that impression would be a great mistake, since it is chemical discoveries as enshrined in chemists' categories that concern us here, rather than just the words they use for marking their distinctions—so a rather different example may help to bring out the point. A man who sets out on a detailed and exhaustive survey of the Polar regions will encounter all sorts of practical difficulties. Some of these are so great as to make the task at present an impossible one to complete; still, there is room to talk of finding a way of doing it some day, given suitable equipment and sufficient grit and determination. This is a nice example of a practical impossibility, the sort which might one day be, but has not yet been, overcome. Someone, however, may point out that the task involves further difficulties and impossibilities which no such equipment and determination can get over. 'Suppose you have been able to make all the observations you require,' he may say, 'even then your difficulties are not over. For, adopting Mercator's projection, you will still not be able to produce your map. Just as Baffin Land comes out large and Greenland larger still, so each mile further north you survey will take up more paper; and, however large you make your map, you will never be able to show the North Pole on it. And this is no mere practical obstacle which we may hope to get over some day: it is a theoretical impossibility, and there's no room to say, "Perhaps some day we'll do it".'

Still, this impossibility is again nothing to worry about—nothing 'unpleasant' that needs 'facing'. For if we chose we could map the same region to a different projection, and then the North Pole would appear on the map in the same way as any other place on the earth's surface. In this case, therefore, the theoretical impossibilities are not more difficult, not even infinitely more difficult to overcome than the practical ones. To speak of difficulty here at all is to misconstrue theoretical impossibilities as a specially obstinate variety of practical ones; whereas all talk of fatalism, of hope deferred, vain attempts or resignation would be a sign of misunderstanding. A theoretical impossibility is not a challenge, so philosophical attitudes are out of place.

What application has this argument to the story of the Running-Down Universe? The suggestion was that the

Second Law of Thermodynamics had apocalyptic implications for two reasons: first, because it applied to the whole universe, and secondly, because it represented a theoretical, and so ineluctable necessity in events. But even if, given its more abstract, theoretical interpretation, the Second Law were applicable to the universe-as-a-whole, would it yet have the consequences depicted? Only if the necessities and impossibilities it told us of were (as is implied) infinitely hard practical ones. This assumption, we can now see, is also highly questionable. Principles of this degree of abstraction may be expected to belong to the conceptual scaffolding of a scientific theory, and the necessities and impossibilities they state will be (so to speak) built into the theory. The phenomena being what they are, we have, no doubt, built up the theories we have for very good reasons. But to say, for instance, 'Processes cannot be weighed, substances can', is not to state these reasons: it is to presuppose them.

It seems fair to suggest that the same conclusion applies to the Second Law itself. There is one crucial test: if there is anything in the implied parallel between theoretical principles of physics and cartographical principles of projection, we shall be free to shift from one set of principles to another at will, provided only we are prepared to accept all the consequential changes in the details of our theories and concepts. So it should be possible, in principle, to adopt in place of the Second Law another law which does not seem to imply a permanent long-term trend in the course of the universe's history: this would be like shifting from Mercator's projection to another projection—one that does not seem to imply that the North and South Poles have a peculiar status, which sets them apart from all other points on the earth's surface, viz. that of unmappability.

Can this be done? One thing has to be said at once: that working physicists have no reason to be dissatisfied with the existing structure of thermodynamics, and so have had little motive for investigating this question. There are no phenomena which a revised thermodynamics would accommodate which cannot be explained within the existing framework of theory. (The reason for choosing one map projection rather than another is not usually that one projection leaves unmapped areas that can be mapped on the other.) The question has, however, been studied by Professor Herbert Dingle, who concludes that the transformation is possible; the laws of heat transfer can, with sufficient ingenuity, be framed in an alternative way which does not involve any suggestion of 'universal thermal decay'. What is perhaps significant is that, if this is done, we can unify heat theory and dynamical theory only by introducing into mechanics itself something akin to the existing entropy law.[5] One can, it seems, start constructing physical theory either with mechanics or with heat theory: whichever way one starts, one will be free of any apparent implication of decay, until one crosses into the other subject. How can it, then, be argued that universal decay is a theoretical necessity inherent either in thermal or in mechanical *phenomena*? Surely the more natural conclusion to draw is that the source of the so-called 'universal tendency to disorganization' lies elsewhere—perhaps in the analogies we have to employ in order to accommodate either the concepts of thermodynamics in a generalized theory of mechanics, or those of mechanics in a generalized theory of thermodynamics.

Let me sum up this long argument. People have thought that we could read the Second Law of Thermodynamics as telling us about the ultimate fate of the universe. So long as physicists accepted the law as a theoretical principle of universal application, it seemed to follow that the universe must be running down. This being so, it was felt (understandably) that we must do something to reconcile ourselves to the ultimate doom; though whether we were to take it heroically, cheerfully or in an other-worldly spirit people could not agree. But the argument is open to criticism on two counts. If we take the Second Law at the phenomenological level, at which it relates most directly to the facts of heat-transfer, the

---

[5] Herbert Dingle, *Through Science to Philosophy*, Ch. 11; and also his contribution to the symposium, *Albert Einstein, Philosopher-Scientist* (Library of Living Philosophers), Ch. 20, and *The Scientific Adventure*, Ch. 16.

argument works only if we assume that a 'universal' law necessarily applies to 'the universe'—and there turn out to be strong reasons for thinking that the law could not be 'about the universe' in the sense required. Alternatively, if we give the law its most theoretical interpretation, the argument works only if we assume that theoretical impossibility is a sub-species of practical impossibility (namely, the *infinitely* difficult): it is this which gives the Second Law its misleading air of inexorability. But so far as an impossibility might (conceivably) be overcome, it is a practical one; and so far as it is a theoretical one, it has no need of being.

All this is not to say that philosophical attitudes to the universe-as-a-whole are unjustifiable, and cannot be argued about. Perhaps we *should* be stoical about the ultimate fate of all things, or carefree, or other-worldly; and no doubt reasons of some sort can be given in favour of adopting one of these attitudes or another. All we are entitled to say is, that physics does not *oblige* us to adopt one, or indeed any, of these attitudes. The running-down universe is a myth, and we shall discover about the Apocalypse from physics only what we read into the subject.

The pitfalls surrounding the notion of an Apocalypse surround equally the idea of a Beginning of All Things; and if we force our astronomical discoveries and physical theories to tell us about this, we once again run serious risks. It is not that we are liable, in so doing, to take for the truth of the matter propositions which are in fact untrue. The prior and greater risk is that of taking for useful and sensible hypotheses suggestions which turn out on closer study to be vacuous or incoherent.

The situation is complicated for us by the fact that we have some evidence of a genuine long-term trend in the progress of past astronomical history. Though the observations are open to interpretation in a number of ways, it does seem quite likely that the galaxies are getting farther apart from one another, and that if we went back far enough in time they would have been very much closer together than they are now.[6] This conclusion has led some people to make suggestions which are not so much extravagant as unintelligible. We are asked, for instance, to suppose that, when the galaxies which are now separate were all packed into a relatively small space, there was no change, and so, 'if time has a meaning only when there is change', no *time*. 'We can conceive', says the late Astronomer-Royal, 'on one view, of a timeless past while creation slept and nothing changed, and on another of an initial creation and of a beginning of time only a few thousand million years ago'.[7] Now there may undoubtedly be difficulties about applying our familiar conception of time at all straightforwardly to a universe as different from ours as that the astronomers think may have existed a few thousand million years ago—though these difficulties are apparently not serious enough to stop them putting an approximate date to it. But the notorious objections even to *asking* when time began are unaffected by anything the telescopes may show us, and the 'two views' we are offered remain equally mysterious.

Can the views even be kept distinct? It is not clear that they can. They are alleged to differ in this, that the one supposes the phase at which the galaxies were most highly compressed to have followed 'a timeless past when nothing changed', while the other supposes it to have followed . . . nothing. But to talk of a genuinely 'timeless' past, a past 'when time had no meaning', would be to talk in a way which deprived of sense even the proposition that *nothing* changed: if the assertion 'Nothing changed' is to be intelligible, must one not at any rate be able to ask *for how long* this state of affairs continued? So we may wonder whether the choice between 'a timeless past' and no past at all is a genuine choice after all.

Either way, whichever 'view'—or better, whichever form of words—we favour, violence is done to our understandings. We might make something of the hypothesis that, up till a few thousand million years ago, all the matter composing the present galaxies had remained stationary and compressed

6 Cf. G. J. Whitrow, *The Structure of the Universe* (Hutchinson 1949), Ch. 2.
7 *Science News*, No. 32, pp. 23–4.

together for an indefinite time, though what evidence would be required in order to establish that this had been the case is not obvious—certainly none that astronomers now possess would be enough to do so. But to present this indefinitely long unchanging phase as either 'a timeless past' or as 'before time began' is to play, not for understanding, but for mystified acquiescence. Perhaps the phase of maximum compression was the beginning, not only of the current phase of astronomical history, but also of . . . all objects and happenings whatever. But this is hardly the sort of thing which could be proved by resort to the telescope: an event which was logically as unique as a Creation of All Things would not be open to discussion in terms of ordinary induction and analogy. As things stand, we have no reason to suppose that the phase of maximum compression did not have predecessors in a perfectly familiar sense—for all we now know, there may prove to be heavenly bodies, sufficiently distant, which were not involved in the initial 'jam' of galactic matter. If we are to believe anything else, indeed, it can hardly be for astronomical reasons alone. One could not seriously identify this 'jam' with a Creation unless one had outside reasons for thinking that this was justifiable.

What sort of outside reasons could there be? Professor Milne, whose theories Dr Spencer-Jones was popularizing in the passage just quoted, was greatly interested in the question what mathematical 'time-scale' one should use in theorizing about the past history of the galaxies. One of his suggestions was that one might use two alternative scales: one of these would be like the Orthographic map projection, or the physicist's 'absolute' scale of temperature, in being bounded in the direction of the past—on this scale, that is to say, the units would be such that only a finite number of units back from now would be properly describable as past 'times'; the other scale would be more like Mercator's projection, or the 'logarithmic' scale of temperature, in being unbounded—on this alternative scale, any number of units back from the present time would represent a 'time' in the past. So far as pure theory goes, there is no reason why such alternative scales should not be used : difficulties begin only when we try to draw conclusions from this fact. For the choice of a time-scale, in this sense, is a conceptual matter alone. We may make our choice in the light of our discoveries about astronomical history, but the choice itself tells us nothing about history: it is a preliminary matter, like the choice of a projection in cartography. What scale we choose makes no difference to the events we have to chronicle; and the suggestion Milne makes, that the moment of greatest galactic compression might be one and the same as the initial point of his bounded time-scale, is no improvement on the bare hypothesis that this was 'when time began'.

At the present stage in physical cosmology, it is no good our being in a hurry. As in history and archaeology, the only hope of solid results lies in a step-by-step advance. There will always be some point in our map of the past history of the universe beyond which we have nothing particular to show. The same goes for the future—and how could it be otherwise? If we force astrophysics to serve us with a revised version of Genesis and Revelation we dig a pit for ourselves. Suppose we look at the map of an unsurveyed country, we shall find that it is not completely empty, for it will bear at least the parallels of longitude and latitude. But it would be a mistake to think that these, by themselves, told us anything geographical about the surface of the earth; and the same pitfall awaits us in cosmology. However we may argue about our choice of time-scales, these will remain the bare scaffolding of astrophysical theory. The danger is that we may misinterpret them as giving us genuinely historical information.

III

ETHICS AND COSMIC EVOLUTION

THE myths of the past have always had justificatory purposes as well as explanatory ones. They have set out to show people not only how it is that Nature and Society and Man have come to be related as they are, but also why these relations are rightly as they are. To the peoples of the Ancient Near East, a royal genealogy was more than a historical record, it was a warrant—a guarantee of the legitimate authority of their rulers—which related the order of society to the order of nature, usually by crediting the sovereign with a direct line of descent from the creator-gods of the country. The mythical figures of their cosmologies, again, stood in social relationships to one another as much as men did; and the pattern of these relationships commonly reflected the social structure of the community itself, so that it seemed in the nature of things that the social structure should be as it was. Ethical and political issues were thereby given cosmological foundations, the Nature of Things being identified with the Right Order of Things.[1]

This ambition, to find 'a cosmic sanction for ethics', a 'natural foundation on which our human superstructure of right and wrong may safely rest', is an enduring one. We feel there should be some sign in the world of nature which can reassure us that our ideals of society and morality, as they have grown up through the centuries, are enduring and of real worth. Can we not find some parallel between the pattern and progress of society and their counterparts in the rest of nature? Can we not discern some order and direction in the

[1] H. Frankfort et al., *Before Philosophy* (Pelican edn.), give a useful account of this subject.

37

development of things at large? This is a problem any man may think worth tackling.

Scientists have naturally been concerned with this problem as much as anyone else, and have often thought that the results of their professional inquiries could be relied on to provide a solution. To take one example: Aristotle introduced, for purely biological purposes, the idea of a 'scale of nature'—in this scale all things could be ordered, rocks at the foot and men at the head, and each upward step took one farther away from the inert and towards fully living and reasoning creatures. His one point in constructing this scale was to emphasize the continuity between living things and inert ones. Wherever one thought to draw a sharp line across the scale, borderline creatures could be found, so that stones, plants, animals and men could not be classified in entirely separate pigeon-holes, rigidly insulated from one another: there would always be such things as sponges (or in our day viruses) which would blur the divisions in any attempt at a rigid classification.[2] In later times, however, this idea of Aristotle's was given quite a different interpretation. From being an account of the way things were *in fact* related, it became a specification of the hierarchy in which they *ought* to be related. The Scale of Nature became the 'Sovereign Order of Nature'; and now a creature's place in the scale—the extent to which it differed from the entirely inert and approximated towards the ideal of full life and rationality—was made to represent also its 'station' in the Society of Nature. A creature at one level was given 'authority' over those at all lower levels, and was subject in turn to all those above it. Man being at the head of Aristotle's scale, he was set in dominion over the lower creatures; but now Angels were placed above him in the scale, with God in the topmost place of all, man being as much a subject to them as the lower creatures were to him.[3]

Whatever sympathy one has with this view of things, the view is more than a biological one. If we are going to order the creatures of nature in a hierarchy, as opposed to a strictly

[2] C. Singer, *A History of Biology* (Oxford 1931), Ch. I. §11.
[3] E.g. S. Mason, *A History of the Sciences* (1953), pp. 141-2.

taxonomic scheme, this may be as good a way of doing so as any; but the question whether it should be done in this way or some other is not a question which can be determined from biological considerations alone. Suppose someone were to argue, as against this view, that authority in the world of nature should derive from longevity rather than degree of life or rationality: as men among themselves regard their parents and grandparents as entitled to honour and respect, he might say, in the same way all men, as comparatively short-lived creatures, should honour and respect the tortoise, the carp and the elephant. A hierarchy constructed on this principle would differ strikingly from that based on Aristotle's scale—for instance, it would make the rocks of the Western Highlands the most honourable things in the British Isles—yet how could one choose between them? Not on biological grounds alone surely: neither view could be claimed as 'biologically correct' or dismissed as 'biologically unsound'. So if the disputants turned to a biologist to arbitrate between them, he would have to reply as follows: 'In this matter I cannot claim to be an expert. As a biologist I can tell you what sorts of creatures there are, and in what ways they resemble and differ from one another; I can order them for you on different principles, and tell you what principles of classification are the best for the special purposes of my science; but when it comes to what you call "authority" and "respect", you leave my province. The question whether longevity is the most honourable characteristic a creature can have, or rather a high degree of life and rationality, is one which I am at liberty to have views about, but not as a professional. As a matter of fact, my own feeling is . . .'—and here he could go on to tell us his own personal attitude to the question.

The idea of a Sovereign Order of Nature is, in other words, not a purely biological idea: it is an idea originating in biology, but taken over from it and extended to do a fresh, non-biological job. As a matter of biology alone, a creature's place in the scale of nature carries with it no hint of 'authority': to introduce this further element is to elevate the scale of nature out of taxonomy into the realm of scientific mythology. Once this has been done, it has to be recognized that the questions one asks become more than scientific questions— 'for all that experiment or observation can show', we said, 'one scientific myth is as good as another'. Here as elsewhere, the attitude which we should adopt towards nature cannot be settled in the way in which one establishes what the facts of nature are; and, when disputes arise about the proper attitude to adopt, scientific considerations alone will be incompetent to resolve them.

In the last 150 years, biologists have given up the idea that creatures can be arranged in a linear sequence. The scale of nature has gone, and in its place we are offered a vast and complex family-tree, showing the genealogical relations (many of them still hypothetical) between the different species of living creatures. As for geology, that has separated off completely, and scientists no longer hope, as even Linnaeus did, to classify inert objects on the same principles as living things. Yet the idea of a Sovereign Order of Nature is not dead. It has roots elsewhere than in the field of biology, and has survived (though transformed) the revolutions produced in biology by Cuvier, Darwin and their successors. From the old idea that the Scale of Nature was fixed, scientists have turned to the idea of evolution; and the theory of organic evolution has, in its turn, been made the starting-point of new ethico-political myths. These are worth a little examination, for they provide as good an illustration as one could find of the difference between scientific theories and scientific myths.

At the present time, the leading advocate of 'Evolutionary Ethics' is Dr Julian Huxley.[4] For him the object of biological study is not only an understanding of how things are: it is also a recognition of how they ought to be. From discoveries about evolution, from 'the new knowledge amassed by biologists during the last hundred years' (he tells us) we can obtain

---

[4] His own writings on this subject and those of his grandfather T. H. Huxley are conveniently reprinted together in *Evolution and Ethics 1893–1943* (1947): the quotations discussed here are taken chiefly from the Herbert Spencer lecture on 'Evolutionary Ethics'.

'definite guidance as to how we should try to plan social and political change'. When we search for the foundation of ethics, we should look to the biologists' theory of evolution, for the object of one search is to be found in the process of evolutionary development: 'the ultimate guarantees for the correctness of our labels of rightness and wrongness are to be sought for among the facts of evolutionary direction'. What Nature is, and how it has reached its present state, he tells us as a biologist; and from there he goes on in his capacity as a prophet, to tell us both where Nature is going and more . . . that it is our job to help her along.

Can one really draw this sharp distinction between the tasks of a biologist and those of a prophet? Dr Huxley would deny this, and it is my main business to establish, on the contrary, that one can. So with one eye on his text, and the other on my previous argument, let us inquire what sort of connection he is asking us to recognize between the facts and theories of biology and our ethical and political ideals. Does a proper understanding of the theory of evolution dictate to us what our ideals should be? Or is the connection a more tenuous one—does one have to tinker with the results of biological study before they will yield conclusions of this sort? Only in the first case can the biologist speak about ethics in a tone of authority: once he begins to expand or extend biological concepts in ways which are not needed for purposes of explanation, the difficulties we have already encountered will begin to arise—there will no longer be any way of selecting from among all the views that might be put forward one particular 'biologically correct' one.

How then, for Julian Huxley, do the discoveries of biology support ethics? One must assume first that the scientific facts are intended in the ordinary way as *reasons*, and for him conclusive reasons, for selecting certain policies, principles and practices and rejecting others. To this, T. H. Huxley (Julian's own grandfather) would certainly not have agreed. 'Cosmic evolution', he wrote, 'may teach us how the good and evil tendencies in man may have come about; but, in itself, it is incompetent to furnish any better reason why what we call

good is preferable to what we call evil than we had before.'
Still, this is the first possibility we must examine.

If we interpret Julian Huxley in this way, we can give a
summary selection of the backing he offers for his ethical
claims in his own words:

'Evolution, from cosmic star-dust to human society, is a
comprehensive and continuous process. During the process new
and more complex levels of organization are progressively
attained, and new possibilities are thus opened up to the universal
world-stuff. Evolution on the inorganic level operates over an
appalling vastness of space. Finally on our earth the world-stuff
arrived at the new type of organization that we call life. During
the thousand million years of organic evolution, the degree of
organization attained by the highest forms of life increased
enormously. Finally there is, in certain types of animals, an
increase in consciousness or mind. There is thus one direction
within the multifariousness of evolution which we can legitimately call progress. Biological or organic evolution has at its
upper end been merged into and largely succeeded by conscious
or social evolution. It is only through social evolution that the
world-stuff can now realize radically new possibilities. And in so
far as the mechanisms of evolution ceases to be blind and automatic and becomes conscious, ethics can be injected into the
evolutionary process. The evolving world-stuff can now proceed
to some understanding of the cosmos which gave it birth. . . .'

This is heady stuff, and one hesitates before calling it
science. Still, up to this point there is nothing in it of an
unambiguously ethical sort. Later on, however, he is making
undeniably ethical claims:

'Social organization should be planned, not to prevent change,
not merely to permit it, but to encourage it. . . . Social morality
is seen to include the duty of providing an immense extension
of research. . . . Knowledge, love, beauty, selfless morality, and
firm purpose are ethically good. . . . The major ethical problem
of our time is to achieve global unity for man.'

How does he make the transition? The crucial passage in
which the jump from science to ethics is taken is as follows:

'When we look at evolution as a whole, we find, among the many directions which it has taken, one which is characterized by introducing the evolving world-stuff to progressively higher levels of organization and so to new possibilities of being, action, and experience. This direction has culminated in the attainment of a state where the world-stuff (now moulded into human shape) finds that it experiences some of the new possibilities as having value in and for themselves; and further that among these it assigns higher and lower degrees of value, the higher values being those which are more intrinsically or more permanently satisfying, or involve a greater degree of perfection.

'The teleologically-minded would say that this trend embodies evolution's purpose. I do not feel that we should use the word purpose save where we know that a conscious aim is involved; but we can say that this is the *most desirable* direction of evolution, and accordingly that our ethical standards must fit into its dynamic framework. In other words, it is ethically right to aim at whatever will promote the increasingly full realization of increasingly higher values.'

From this passage, one can extract the fundamental ethical principle from which all Dr Huxley's ethical conclusions are presented as following; namely, that 'it is ethically right to aim at whatever will promote the increasingly full realization of those values which are more intrinsically or more permanently satisfying, or involve a greater degree of perfection'. Where does evolution enter into this? It does not come in at all. The reference to this notion, indeed all reference to biology, has dropped out. Regarded as reasons for our choices and preferences, or as premisses of a formal argument, all the statements in the preliminary scientific 'build-up' cancel out before the vital step into ethics. (In any case, one might add—though this is by the way—the principle finally reached is too sloppily stated to be of any genuine help to us: of course the 'rightness' of an action in some way 'involves' the 'degree of perfection' of whatever it 'promotes', but how? To say only this much is to stop at the very point where the real business of philosophical ethics begins.)

Our first hypothesis must therefore be dismissed. However the facts about organic evolution are intended by Dr Huxley to support his ethical views, it is not by serving as 'reasons' for them. When he says that 'any standards of rightness or wrongness must in some way be related to the movement of the evolutionary process through time', the connection he sees between morality and evolution is evidently of another sort. Let us see, then, just what he means by the term 'evolution' in this context, and how this compares with the meaning the word has in strictly biological contexts. 'Here as elsewhere', wrote T. H. Huxley, 'names are noise and smoke; the important point is to have a clear and adequate conception of the fact signified by a name.' So is the 'evolution' which for Dr Huxley has a clear connection with ethics simply the biologist's notion? Or is there, for him, something more to it?

First, a word about the part the notion of evolution plays in science proper. This notion was introduced to account for the way in which the distribution of different biological species changes as time goes on: it is concerned, that is, with the relative success of different stocks of creatures in the competition for survival and multiplication. A corollary of this is, that zoologists do not study some single process called 'evolution'; they study an unlimited number of processes, all of which are equally entitled to be called 'evolutionary processes'. The extinction of the mammoths, the growth in the British fulmar population, the development of the lion from its fossil forbears; these are all evolutionary processes, no more and no less than the process by which our own stock sprang from the early primates. It is, in other words, not a unitary process called 'Evolution' that zoologists study, so much as 'the evolution of this-or-that species in a particular environment from such-a-stock'. (There may of course prove to be close similarities between these different processes, which entitles zoologists to explain many of them as instances of a single *type* of process, but that is another matter.) So the whole theory of evolution is such as an intelligent lion or an articulate ant might subscribe to. Although, as men, we may be more curious than a lion or an ant would be about the details of our own remote ancestry, this particular problem is for the zoologist just one among others. If it raises problems of special theoretical interest, well and good : but for many purposes it is more practical to study fruit-flies.

What sort of implications, then, can the theory of organic evolution have for ethics ? Its subject matter is the external, or foreign relations between each kind of creature and the others with which it is in competition—between the mammoths, for instance, and the creatures that displaced them. The domestic relations between the individuals of a given species are its concern only in special circumstances, if they react upon the survival-value of the stock—if, for instance, it turns out that civil strife among the mammoths was a factor in their disappearance. But even in that case a biologist could say professionally only that this explains how it was that they became extinct, not that it shows that they had been wicked to quarrel. So the idea of natural selection between species and their sub-species and varieties—for which the biological term 'evolution' is an abbreviation—could have a direct relevance to our ethical problems only if the human race were seriously threatened by the rise of, say, a race of giant ants.

But has not the course of evolution a direction ? Is there not as Dr Huxley puts it 'one direction within the multifariousness of evolution which we can legitimately call progress' ? And does this not have ethical significance for us ? Certainly, it is natural enough that one should put the different sorts of creature there are in an order, according to their degree of evolutionary success : such a classification may be of real use to biology. We can, therefore, understand a biologist's choosing to define 'degree of evolutionary advance' in terms of the qualities associated with survival : namely, ability to control the environment, independence of the environment and capacity to develop further in the same direction. But these criteria, which may serve as a test of 'biological progress', have no more to do with morality than the original notion of natural selection. They, too, are concerned with the actual external rather than the proper internal relations of biological species.

It can hardly, therefore, be the working zoologist's notion of evolution that Julian Huxley has in mind when he talks about the relevance of Evolution to Ethics. Nor does he seriously suggest that it is: Darwin's conclusion that the 'ethical yard-stick' is concerned less with evolution, in the sense of natural selection, than with a man's relation to his fellows, Huxley considers a feeble one. For him, 'evolution' means more than natural selection. It is a composite notion and a more grandiose one for which the biological term serves only as a starting-point. Here is the recipe for producing it. First, select from the countless evolutionary processes that biologists study the particular one which has led up to the appearance of man—this puts man in a preferential position, whose justice the lion or the ant might question, but the justification would be man's greater degree of 'evolutionary advance'. Then tack on to the beginning of this historical sequence a series of physico-chemical events leading up to the appearance of the first living creatures, and at the latter end treat the development of civilization and technology as a continuation of the biological trend 'by other means'—in this way, as Huxley puts it, we 'extend the concept of evolution both backward into the inorganic and forward into the human domain'. Finally, christen your conceptual artefact 'the cosmic process' and present it as a golden thread leading from the remotest past up to the present day and on into the future. This, not 'evolution' in the pure biologist's sense, is the touchstone Julian Huxley offers for solving our ethical problems.

Can the composite notion constructed to this recipe claim to be a genuine scientific notion? It could do, if the extended use of the term were forced on us by the facts—that is, if we needed to appeal to it in order to explain the occurrence of events which must otherwise remain unexplained. But the motive for extending the meaning of the word 'evolution' as Huxley encourages us to do, is not to explain anything fresh: it is something very different.

We find here both of the features characteristic of a scientific myth. The key-term used has to be understood, not in its straight scientific sense, but in an extended one; and this extension is made for other than scientific motives—so that, when differences of opinion arise, there is, scientifically.

46

speaking, no longer any way of deciding between them. We are to use the term 'evolution' to cover not only biological processes, but also certain inorganic phenomena which took place before the appearance of living creatures on the earth and, in addition, the development of human society since the emergence of man. This means giving the term 'evolution' a very different shape from its zoological one, and forcing it into quite a fresh jig-saw. The claim that biology is behind Huxley's ethical claims cannot therefore be allowed; and once we start changing the meaning of the term 'evolution', to put it to non-scientific tasks, biology can no longer resolve our difficulties when incompatible views are put forward.

There are in my case ambiguities about the recipe: the zoological sequence of events leading up to the appearance of man may be determinate enough, but which exactly are 'the' inorganic processes leading up to the appearance of the first living organisms? How are we to select these favoured processes from all those taking place 'over the appalling vastness of space' a million years before the first cells formed? Even worse, what criteria are we to use to select 'the' process of social development, except by begging the very ethical questions that Evolution was going to help us to solve? The biological criteria of 'degree of evolutionary advance' are hardly enough, for emphasis on 'control over and independence of environment' suggests that technological skill is the sole criterion of social advance. Yet if we add further criteria and judge social progress on other grounds, we cannot help being influenced by our own ethical preferences when we make our selection.

Once this stage is reached, the impossibility of selecting between ethical views on biological grounds becomes absolute. For now, so far from our finding the ultimate guarantees for the correctness of our labels of rightness and wrongness among 'the facts of evolutionary development', the present-day direction of that development becomes itself a matter of opinion. The question 'Which way is Evolution moving to-day?' now becomes equivalent to the question, 'Which way *ought* society to develop to-day?': the appearance of biological fact simply conceals the ethical character of the point at issue. Restoring horse and cart to their proper positions, we now have to look for the ultimate guarantees of our generalized labels of 'evolution' and 'evolutionary progress' among the facts of morality. Having extended the notion of evolution into the moral sphere we can no longer decide unambiguously what Evolution is, unless we have already *settled* our ethical disagreements.

Again, as we foresaw, when different views about the relevance of evolution to ethics are put forward by other writers, there proves scientifically to be no way of choosing between their views and Julian Huxley's. He is certainly not the only man who invites us to think of the history of the universe in this way : we all know of others who represent the development of the cosmos as, so to speak, the progress of a cosmic band-waggon—a historical juggernaut sweeping irresistibly out of the past and on into the future. It is not surprising to find that Hegelian and Marxist theorists, too, include biological evolution as one phase in their 'dialectical process'. But whichever account of the 'cosmic process' we look at, the same difficulties arise the moment one tries to draw concrete morals from it. For instance, ought we to jump on to the waggon and travel with it, or ought we to try to stop it? And if we ought to jump on to it, what is its destination? In each case there are several opinions, and even those who advocate jumping on the waggon disagree about its route. Hegel thought the King of Prussia was at the wheel, but this view is now implausible; nowadays dialecticians do not always agree whether the main line goes through Moscow or through Belgrade; while Julian Huxley would prefer to think the waggon called at the United Nations Headquarters. But how can we settle which of them is right?

There are also those who would have us put the waggon into reverse. T. H. Huxley himself is a good example—'The ethical progress of society depends,' he wrote, 'not on imitating the cosmic process, still less on running away from it, but on combating it.' Between him and Julian there is therefore a flat contradiction. Can we choose between their views? Not on scientific grounds; for the question, whether social and moral progress are to be regarded as a continuation of the process of natural selection or as a reaction against it, is not one which can be answered by appeal to observations or experiments. There is no question of phenomena turning up one day which could be accounted for only on one or the other of the two views, as would have to be the case if the issue were really a scientific one.

What is the real point at issue, then? If we ask this, we shall see the nature of Evolution Myths more clearly. When one considers why each of the two Huxleys chooses to 'extend' the notion of evolution as he does, the most one can find is a difference of temper between them; there is no disagreement about the facts. One of them sees social development as a continuation of the process of natural selection, the other as a reversal of it; and these different attitudes to 'evolution' reflect the different things they want to do with the notion.

For Thomas Henry Huxley, 'evolution' represented a Challenge: for Julian it is a Talisman. T.H. was concerned to point out important differences between the methods of natural selection and of social and moral development. What struck him about natural selection was the starvation and slaughter through which species supplant one another, and especially the fate of the weak and the meek. This brutality, he felt, was just the thing which, in our relations with our fellow human beings, we must fight against. He therefore painted a picture of Man as pitted against Nature, and turned his spotlight on to the competitive aspect of biological evolution, contrasting the brutality and destructiveness of natural selection with the harmony desirable in society and by implication criticizing a political economy of unrestricted competition.

'The struggle for existence tends to eliminate those less fitted to adapt themselves to the circumstances of their existence. The strongest, the most self-assertive, tend to tread down the weaker. But the influence of the cosmic process on the evolution of society is the greater the more rudimentary its civilization. Social progress means a checking of the cosmic process at every step and the substitution for it of another, which may be called the ethical process; the end of which is not the survival of those which may happen to be the fittest, in respect of the whole of the conditions which obtain, but of those who are ethically the best.'

T. H. Huxley, in other words, used the devilish mechanism of natural selection as material for a parable—'Nature red in tooth and claw' was to do duty as a symbol of our own competitive brutality. For these purposes, one must agree, the 'cosmic process' was well fitted to play the part of the Devil.

When Julian Huxley writes about his 'Evolutionary Ethics', however, he is not interested in producing a parable directed against cruelty and selfishness. So far from spoiling for a fight with nature, he feels it most important to have Nature behind him. T. H. Huxley saw in the cosmic process an enemy worth fighting, and set his great bearded jaw against it: Julian turns to the same process for reassurance. The connection he sees between evolution and ethics is not, after all, a logical or scientific one. What he is looking for, he says, is 'reassurance' in the face of a 'hatefully imperfect world'; a 'cosmic sanction for ethics', a 'natural foundation on which our human superstructure of right and wrong may safely rest'—in a phrase, *ein' feste Burg*. His aim being different, he casts the cosmic process in a different role: we are to think of Evolution not as the Devil but rather as the Deity.

Once this is recognized, a great deal becomes clear which was formerly mysterious. The tone in which he writes, for instance, is so unlike the cold, scrupulous tone of a learned scientific journal:

'Compared with what a protozoan or a polyp can show, the complexity of later forms of life, like bee or swallow or antelope, is stupendous, their capacity for self-regulation almost miraculous, their experience so much richer and more varied as to be different in kind.'

This is the sort of writing one expects rather in Paley's *Natural Theology*. Indeed, whenever Dr Huxley writes about this topic, one keeps coming across passages written in the language of wonder, not of theory—of religion, not of science—passages designed (in Pascal's phrase) 'to enkindle, not to instruct'.

To do Dr Huxley justice, he has no serious intention of disguising the theological character of his writing, for his account of Evolution is openly presented as the theology of his own 'Religion without Revelation'. It is only because he is a scientist that one at first expects his writings to belong to popular science, rather than theology. Yet this is a mistake which could really have been made only in the twentieth century: until our own time, scientists have always been accustomed to writing on natural theology, and to using the scientific discoveries they described for theological ends. Evolution, then, takes on for Dr Huxley most of the jobs of the discredited Deity:

'The so-called immutable laws and will of God, which are invoked to guarantee the principles of ethics, turn out to have been extremely changeable; and the principles of ethics have changed with them.'

God has failed: we must therefore put our trust in Evolution, and vary our ethical beliefs as it directs. Evolution now becomes not only the Source of Comfort and Reassurance—'evolutionary ethics is of necessity a hopeful ethics'; it figures also as the Immanent and Omnipresent Creator, that 'comprehensive and continuous process' which 'moulded the world-stuff into human shape', and whose Agent it is man's privilege to be—'Man is not only the heir of the past and the victim of the present: he is also the agent through whom evolution may unfold its further possibilities.' All the wonders which for Archdeacon Paley were evidences of the existence of God can on this view be put to the credit of Evolution. As for us, we can be confident that the direction in which it is going is the right one; so, if only we mount the waggon, all will be for the best.

Now it is not my purpose to criticize these views from the point of view of theology: I am content with showing that this is what they are. Yet there are several drawbacks to a religion of Evolution which even a layman will feel. To begin with, it must be a religion of limited appeal, seeing that the Myths on which it is based are expressed in a way properly intelligible only to professional biologists—for others the analogy between moral progress and biological progress will have no great force. Again, the Supreme Being it presents to us is hardly an object of respect: Dr Huxley himself calls it 'a glorious paradox' that 'this purposeless mechanism, after a thousand million years of its blind and automatic operations, has finally generated purpose' now that 'Man the conscious microcosm has been thrown up by the blind and automatic forces of the unconscious macrocosm'. Worst of all, perhaps, it is not a religion with much power to stimulate human endeavour; for those who have not sufficient scientific training to recognize the limited scope of the analogy between moral and biological development (that is to say, for most of us) its effect would probably be just the opposite. This was certainly the effect of its Hellenistic counterpart, the religion of $T\acute{v}\chi\eta$, the personification of chance, which had a vogue after the Olympian Gods had become discredited.

All that matters for my present argument is the logical point, that the two Huxleys' conclusions about the relevance of biological evolution to ethics are not themselves scientific conclusions. Logically speaking, there is no reason why you should not hold either position—or both. There is a good deal in what they both say, and which aspect of the theory of evolution you could consider the more worth stressing will depend on your immediate aim and interests. This aim may be partly a matter of temperament: one could write an essay contrasting the attitudes of T. H. Huxley's two author-grandsons—J. S. cheerfully accepting biology and progress, Aldous critical of both. (The character of Shearwater in *Antic Hay* would make a natural starting-point.) Partly it will be a matter of historical circumstances: we in the mid-twentieth century have had enough brutality to contend with nearer home for us not to worry, like T. H. Huxley, about the brutality of natural selection, while, conversely, there would have seemed less need sixty years ago for the kind of comfort that the Cosmic Process affords Julian Huxley now. Whichever position you choose, one thing alone is essential: not to suppose that there is any material conflict between the positions or conclude, as Julian Huxley does, that 'T. H. Huxley's antithesis between ethics and evolution was false'. In this context, the word 'false' is far too strong. What we are called on to decide is not which of two scientific theories is better in accord with the facts of observation: the task is now to decide in which of two Scientific Myths we find the more congenial attitude to Nature.

Several questions about Julian Huxley's account of the matter are, however, still unanswered. He is evidently reassured by the thought that the 'cosmic process' is at hand to serve as a 'foundation' for ethics. Yet how does this come about? Supposing ethics to need a prop, how could evolution serve as one? It is not clear in what sense the one can be said to 'support' the other, and the sceptical might ask whether evolution provided a genuine foundation for ethics any more than a row of whisky-drinkers genuinely propped up a bar.

Of course, the intellectual support of science is nowadays worth claiming for any position, however tenuous your justification. One remembers how the impressionist painters, too, claimed that their techniques were more scientific than those of their predecessors had been. If olive and brown and purple were not in the spectrum, they argued, painters should not allow them on their canvases, and only pure colours, the colours of the spectrum, should be used. Yet, however admirable the results of the impressionists' decision, however fruitful the technical experiments they were inspired by their reading of physical optics to make, the idea that the discoveries of physics could *justify* their techniques was an illusion. A painter may *choose* to use only the colours of the spectrum, but it will be by his works, not by science, that his choice will be justified. Whether the impressionists succeeded in their aim only a beholder is in a position to say—the purity of their colour is a matter, not for the spectroscope, but for the eye.

Is it in this sense that we are to think of evolution as justifying ethics? Is the motive behind the suggestion simply a wish to see some connection, however far-fetched, between the workings of nature and the principles of morals? There is, I think, more to be said. In some ways, the myth of Evolution is like the Atlas myth: both, to stress the obvious, proffer support in contexts in which no support is needed. But both also have deeper motives which are worth uncovering. Atlas, for instance, is often thought of as showing only how ignorant the Ancients were: had they known a little more about the solar system, we feel, they would have seen that there was no need for an Atlas, for he was the answer to the question 'What holds the Earth up?', a question which need never arise. Yet surely Atlas was the product not merely of ignorance. There were a vast number of things besides the mechanism of the solar system of which the Ancients were ignorant; but very few of them gave rise to myths. Only where this ignorance was of importance, where it seemed to mean insecurity, was a myth born. Whether or no we have a clear and satisfactory picture of the solar system may not matter to us directly, for after all there are few ways in which we make direct use of this understanding. It is, however, by their indirect effects that myths get hold on us, and in this case the effects are considerable, so that one is not surprised to find that Atlas has counterparts in many mythologies. The stability of the Earth becomes a symbol for so much else. If we have no assurance of that, what else can we trust? No better outlet could be found for 'an anxious fear of future events'; there could be no guarantees, no reassurance about the future, without the confidence that the ground below our feet rested on good, strong shoulders.

Similar motives are probably at work in generating Evolution myths. The support given by Evolution to ethics serves as a source of confidence in our moral ideas, rather than as an intellectual justification of them. In a time of uncertainty and change it is natural for us to wonder whether, in doing what we think right, we may not simply be wasting our time; as a result, we may feel the need of some assurance that there is (so to speak) some future in ethics. People become unhappy about the prospects of virtue paying any dividends, and begin to look elsewhere for a security. This may, intellectually, be as much the result of a misconception as the demand for an Atlas to hold up the Earth—I think myself it is. Still, quite apart from intellectual questions, there is a further point. If you can paint a picture of social and moral development as being all of a piece with biological development, this may help you to feel that morality is something long-standing and of proved worth, something with roots in the universe and no mere human makeshift. Then next time you feel the fear that morality may after all not prove a paying proposition, you can at least (on this view) comfort yourself with the thought that such an ancient institution as the cosmic process is not likely to default.

An anxious fear that the Earth itself may be insecure: that is what gives the Atlas myth its strength. The same kinds of motives can be seen behind many of the old stories. Fear of the sea and the storm, fear of the harvest failing, and the hope of averting these calamities by propitiation: these, not mere ignorance, were responsible for Poseidon, Wotan and Ceres. The same motives remain strong, even though our ignorance may be less. An anxious fear of the remote and unknown past, and of the remote and even more unknown future: these lead us to look for eschatological morals even where there is no hope of finding them—in physical cosmology. Again, the desire that morality should unquestionably be worth while, that the importance to us of our own affairs should find a reflection through all the history of the universe: is it fanciful to see this as the motive behind the Myths of Evolution?

My most serious doubt is whether biological prose, however highly coloured, could ever be an adequate medium for putting this desire into words. It is perhaps inevitably a poetical desire, this impulse to read our purposes into the world of nature. To find the essence of virtue, not in the day-to-day give-and-take of domestic life, but embedded somewhere in the impersonal structure of things: that would be to discover a true Talisman; and the writers who have captured the impulse most successfully have done so in a prose which was very near to poetry. Here is how Virginia Woolf put it, in *To the Lighthouse*:

'As summer neared, as the evenings lengthened, there came to the wakeful, the hopeful, walking the beach, stirring the pool, imaginations of the strangest kind—of flesh turned to atoms which drove before the wind, of stars flashing in their hearts, of cliff, sea, cloud and sky brought purposely together to assemble outwardly the scattered vision within. In those mirrors, the minds of men, in those pools of uneasy water, in which clouds for ever turn and shadows form, dreams persisted, and it was impossible to resist the strange intimation which every gull, flower, tree, man and woman, and the white earth itself seemed to declare (but if questioned at once to withdraw) that good triumphs, happiness prevails, order rules; or to resist the extraordinary stimulus to range hither and thither in search of some absolute good, some crystal of intensity, remote from the known pleasures and familiar virtues, something alien to the processes of domestic life, single, hard, bright, like a diamond in the sand, which would render the possessor secure.'

IV

SCIENCE AND OUR VIEW OF THE WORLD

THE ambassadors of the intellect in high places often express their regret at the 'divorce' between natural science on the one hand and philosophy on the other. In it they see not just an intellectual lacuna—the sort of thing which one would like to see filled, for reasons of disinterested curiosity alone, like the blanks in an all-but-completed cross-word puzzle. To them the divorce appears a sign, a symptom, perhaps even the cause of greater evils and more radical distresses. What the scientist and the philosopher should aim at, they suggest, is a reunion of their disciplines: a 'synthesis' is called for of the results of the special sciences, and this synthesis is to provide a more comprehensive 'world-view' than can be obtained from any one of the special sciences alone.

The response of working scientists and philosophers to this request must be a disappointment. Attempts at reconciliation lead for the most part to mutual suspicion, and it becomes clear that the re-marriage cannot hope to be a love-match. To most scientists 'the acquisition of knowledge about the world of experience' seems sufficient intellectual exercise: this, they declare, is a field 'wide, rich enough in changing hues and patterns to allure us to explore it in all directions'—the 'dry tracts of metaphysics' beyond they willingly leave to others.[1] It is true that some scientists, a few, do set out on the quest for a synthesis, but to their colleagues these activities are, more often than not, an embarrassment.

The indifference is requited. In the years which have passed since G. E. Moore attacked Herbert Spencer's views

---

[1] Max Born, *Atomic Physics* (Blackie 1937), p. 258.

57

on ethics in *Principia Ethica*, professional philosophers (in England at any rate) have hardly felt that philosophy in Spencer's manner—synthetic philosophy, to use his own phrase—was worth serious attention. They have of course felt bound to review, as they appeared, the philosophical writings of Spencer's successors, men such as Huxley, Waddington, Eddington and Jeans; but they have had no difficulty in detecting in all their works enough linguistic confusion and logical sloppiness to dispose of them, at any rate to the satisfaction of the reviewers.

Yet, though spurned by the comrades on either side, the bridge-builders themselves have not felt disposed of. They refuse to agree that Moore's devastating broadsides have found their mark: all they will concede is slight damage to some outlying bastion. Here is Dr Waddington, for instance, on 'the melancholy fate of Herbert Spencer':

'Poor Spencer! He was cajoled or bamboozled by literary men into behaving as though he was talking not about phenomena but about forms of words. Rather half-heartedly he stated, or implied, that what he meant by "good" was "productive of pleasure"; and the critics (e.g. Moore) showed their gratitude at not being asked to raise their eyes from their books by pointing out that that would not do at all.'[2]

The situation is a peculiar one. It is not a question, as one might at first suppose, of whether this activity of 'bridge-building' is being well or ill performed: the question is rather, whether or no the activity gets one anywhere, what it is directed towards, whether it is more than an elaborate intellectual game. Evidently the synthetic philosophers themselves have no doubts: they feel that their activity is both legitimate and important, and the standard lines of philosophical criticism, they claim, are simply irrelevant. If this claim is just, the consequences are important: the professional philosophers have missed the point, and have failed to recognize what the bridge-builders are about. Why,

[2] C. H. Waddington, *Science and Ethics* (1942), pp. 136-7.

then, have the synthetic philosophers felt so unfairly treated? And why have the professional philosophers, for their part, been so contemptuous of 'bridge-building'? The material we have been looking at in this essay will help us to answer these questions, and to see more clearly the scope and limitations of any world-view synthesized from the conceptions of the natural sciences.

'It is not words the synthetic philosopher is interested in', we are told: 'it is *phenomena*. He is not concerned to frame definitions but rather to see the world aright. Success for him would be represented not by an impeccable analysis of the term "good" but by a proper picture of the order of nature and of man's place in it.' This of course is an entirely laudable programme and, if philosophers had not so much evidence of the harm done in the course of such inquiries by unwittingly accepting bizarre definitions of 'good', there would be nothing to question in the statement of it. It is when we leave programmes and try to get down to business that trouble starts.

What, for instance, is our test of a 'proper' picture of things? Is there a single criterion of 'propriety' capable of general application? Or will the criterion depend on an author's precise intentions, and vary with them? If one is building up a world-view from scientific bricks, we must expect the last to be the case. Synthetic philosophers do not all have the same aims. It is not the hypothetico-deductive explanation or mathematical representation of phenomena which is their aim, nor are our expectations their target. They wish rather to alter our attitudes to all sorts of things, and each author has in this respect his own preoccupations. Even when they seem to be discussing the same subject, such as 'the connection between evolution and ethics', their arguments may (as we saw) have completely disparate intentions; and in consequence there is no question of a final decision between them, no definite test—in the laboratory or elsewhere—on the basis of which one view can be established and an ostensibly opposed view ruled out. That is what makes it so inappropriate to talk in this context of truth and falsity, in any black and white kind of way. When synthetic philosophy is under discussion, we have instead to talk in terms of 'seeing the point of' one doctrine, and 'recognizing that there is something in' or 'being in sympathy with' another. In this field, black-and-white logical judgments have no place.

These conclusions apply with particular force to the world-views which are sometimes produced as 'following from' the different branches of science. If there is no final choice to be made between different views about the relation between ethics and evolution, how much less can we talk about a genuine contradiction between (for example) what people call the 'physical' and 'biological' pictures of the universe.

It is true that, if you confine your attention to the materials of one single branch of science at a time, you will be able to construct from the different sciences world-views, or views of Nature, so completely opposed in temper that they seem impossible to reconcile. The optimistic picture of evolution as a steadily-advancing process, and the pessimistic one of man as engaged in a rearguard action to stem the rising tide of entropy: it is no wonder that Mr John Heath-Stubbs cannot help feeling that these 'must seem to be contradictory, at any rate to our limited intelligence'.[3] None the less, they are not so much contradictory as complementary: to treat the contrast between them as anything stronger is to misunderstand the relation between the expressions of these visions of Nature and the 'scientific evidence' offered in their support. Do the physicist's discoveries justify gloom, and the biologist's hope? This seems to be the implication of the term 'contradictory', and it is a false one. For, if to the outsider there appears to be an air of burgeoning optimism about the science of life which that lifeless subject, physics, so notably lacks, the reason does not lie in anything that physicists and biologists have *discovered*. What is relevant here is, rather, the distinction we ourselves have drawn between 'physics' on the one hand and 'biology' on the other—the manner in which we have come to sort out the subject-matter and methods to be labelled 'physical' from those which are to be called 'biological'. This

[3] *Poems of Leopardi*, tr. Heath-Stubbs (Lehmann 1946), Introduction, p. 13.

preliminary act of ours, not anything scientists have found out subsequently, is what makes biology such a fruitful source of imagery for the optimists, and physics an inexhaustible well for the pessimist.

The point is worth following up a little way; so consider how we do make this selection, and in particular how we tell an 'organism' when we see one. The most striking and characteristic feature of organisms, the thing which marks them off from 'inert' matter, is their activity. Teleological words, words referring to 'conduct', apply only to living things, and in their literal and original senses do not make sense of the inert. What goes on under the skin may be interesting and important but it is, from the logical point of view, accidental. Take Mrs Jones' dog Fido and change, as much as you please, his bones and muscles, brain and stomach: provided he still wags his tail for her in the old enchanting way, comes to heel when his mistress calls, eats the joint and barks at Scotsmen, she will feel that she can justly say 'That's the same old Fido'.

The biologist, it is true, soon becomes as interested in the structure of organisms as in their activity. Teleological accounts of their behaviour he comes to regard as a second-best, for he would like to be able to connect up everything in an animal's conduct with his knowledge of its internal structure: in this way it ceases to be Fido and his ways so much as the concentration of phosphorus in his nerves that becomes important. None the less, it is still organisms in whose structure the biologist is interested; and it remains the activity of organisms which is their chief defining characteristic. By 'signs of life' we mean not structures, for these are shared with fossils and the dead, but activities; and however mechanistic a biologist may be in his methods (and very properly so) it is still the structure of *living* matter whose mode of functioning he studies. His subject-matter, in other words, is still pre-selected as coming from the sorts of things which can meaningfully be said to do, want, hunt for, attack and eat things. By contrast, the subject-matter from which the physicist starts consists of the entirely inert, i.e. of those things to which teleological words are least of all applicable.

It is this division of the sciences, according to their methods, the questions they ask and the subject-matter they study, which lies behind the notion that physics and biology imply opposed 'world views'. There is no need for physicists or biologists to make any discoveries about the world in order for this opposition to be established: it was built in to the terms 'physical' and 'biological' in the first place. Nor does the division correspond to any necessary division of scientists by temperament: not all biologists are optimists, nor are all physicists gloomy. For many scientific purposes it is irrelevant whether a specimen is living or lifeless—these are the ones we have chosen to call 'physical'; but if, when a physicist weighs eggs, he does not ask whether they are fertile or addled, it does not follow that he takes them all to be addled. So biologists and physicists have not come respectively to the conclusions that the world is a cheerful or a gloomy place: it is we who have beforehand allotted them their respective fields of study.

All the same, though the idea of physics and biology 'implying' opposed world-views may be a misunderstanding, there is another, more authentic contrast between the sciences. The poet or philosopher who, like Leopardi, sees Man as separate from Nature will find in physics the imagery to express his vision of things since (simply because physics is. physics) it contains no way of referring to the desires, aspirations and aims of men. To introduce references to these things would be to leave the field of physics—by definition, so to say. The physicist's world, then, is to the poet's eye a 'dead' world, a world characterized by 'the destructive potency latent in the volcano, and the vast empty spaces through which wander the lifeless and purposeless stars'.[4]

It becomes clear, however, that physics is being used merely as a source of imagery if we notice the queerness, in this context, of calling the stars 'lifeless and purposeless'. The man who walks so happily along the cliff-top slips and falls to the beach below: the doctor examines his body and

[4] Heath-Stubbs, *loc. cit.*

pronounces it 'lifeless'. The craftsman, skilled through years of practice and absorbed in his work, loses his job in an economic upheaval: he draws his dole and wanders round the streets 'purposeless'. If the words 'lifeless' and 'purposeless' have the meanings and the (depressing) associations they do, it is because they have acquired them in just such contexts as these. Those things are, in this sense, lifeless, which might have been alive but are not; and those purposeless which might be intent on a fruitful goal, but are not. As for the stars, it is not in this sense that they are lifeless and purposeless: they no more resemble a man who has just lost his life or his job than they do a living and busy one. They are, one might more properly say, neither living nor lifeless and neither purposeful nor purposeless; since there seems to us nowadays no way of applying to such things as the stars either of these two oppositions.

Have we, then, any cause to lament? Surely not: if astronomers were, on the other hand, to start treating the heavenly bodies as living creatures once more, we should then begin to have some reason for worrying. Not the least of the merits which Edmund Halley saw in Newton's theory was its power to banish anxieties of this sort:

> 'Now we know
> The sharply veering ways of comets, once
> A source of dread, nor longer do we quail
> Beneath appearances of bearded stars.'[5]

The inertness of the stars—the only sort of 'lifelessness' that can be attributed to them—is surely preferable to their possible malignancy: to lament about it is simply to project one's own despair on to the skies.

As the subject-matter of physics provides the imagery of despair, so that of biology provides the imagery of hope. The biologist's business is with the living, with things that are pursuing many and achieving some ends, desiring much and fulfilling some of their desires; and this preoccupation he shares with the optimistic poets and philosophers, who think

[5] Newton, *Principia* (Cajori edition), p. xiv.

of Man, not as standing apart from, and pitted against Nature, but as one with all her works. But again this does not imply that for the biologist everything is going up and up and on and on!

The logical relation between the arguments presented in support of the 'physical' and 'biological' visions of Nature and the visions themselves is, therefore, the reverse of what it at first sight appears to be. If the doctrines that 'we are powerless to stop the Universe running down' and that 'we are an integral part of the creative process of Evolution' were straight scientific theories, the arguments supporting them would, logically speaking, be reasons for accepting them. The opposition in temper would be accompanied by oppositions of fact. This however is not the situation. The evidence and arguments brought forward in support of one doctrine or the other are not what justifies us in accepting or rejecting it: rather it is the temper of each doctrine which determines what selection of 'evidence' will be presented or spotlighted. Whether you are to accept either doctrine, either vision of Nature, either set of arguments, depends not on the quality of the reasoning, but on how your own attitude to the world already compares with that of the author.

If you are a political optimist, you may be attracted by such lyrical passages as this of Dr Needham's:

'The new world order of social justice and comradeship, the rational and classless world state, is no wild idealistic dream, but a logical extrapolation from the whole course of evolution, having no less authority than that behind it, and therefore of all faiths the most rational.... Even so gigantic a setback [as World War II] cannot shake a faith which is based on the considerations which convinced Drummond and Spencer, Engels and Marx. The way may be long and we may not live to see, but the triumph of the rational spiritual man is sure.'[6]

If however you are a congenital pessimist, you may feel more sympathy for Ostwald's insistence (cited in part earlier in this essay) that

6 J. S. Needham, *Time, the Refreshing River* (Allen & U. 1943), p. 41.

'We must in all circumstances learn to accept the fact that at some indefinite but far-off time our civilization is doomed to go under; that the final purpose of human effort lies in Man himself alone; that it is directed towards his transitory existence; and that, in the longest run, the sum of all human endeavour has no recognizable significance.'[7]

But in neither case will you be presenting scientific conclusions, and there is no question of producing experiments which will finally establish the correctness of one view of Nature and finally torpedo the other.

The fundamental difficulty about 'syntheses' of the sciences is, in the last resort, the difficulty about all scientific myths. So long as scientific concepts and doctrines are employed to explain and represent natural phenomena, we can keep some sort of logical control over what is said: arguments and conclusions are open to criticism and verification—and, as Dr Popper is probably right to emphasize, *falsification*. But when we use terms of a scientific origin in an extended manner, as the vehicles of some more-than-scientific attitude to the world, science is neutral between all conclusions. Even H. G. Wells' characters, under the imminent threat of annihilation by a comet, had a choice of attitudes—in similar circumstances, we ourselves would no doubt go, some to the pub, some to the church, and some to continue digging our gardens, and no one of these reactions would be either more or less 'scientific' than the other two.

So perhaps the unwillingness of working philosophers and scientists to consider a re-marriage of their disciplines is, after all, justifiable. Perhaps the demand for a synthesis is, to say the least, premature, and perhaps 'visions of Nature', as opposed to theories about the workings of natural things, are best left to the poets. Certainly Dr Needham cannot compare, as a spokesman for optimism, with Wordsworth; and the gloomy chemist, Professor Ostwald, can do no more than echo the despairing lament of Leopardi on the barren slopes of Vesuvius:

7 F. W. Ostwald, *Die Philosophie der Werte*, p. 98.

'Gaze and see
How loving Nature cares
For our poor human race, and learn to value
At a just estimate the strength of Man,
Whom the harsh Nurse, even when he fears it least,
With a slight motion does in part destroy,
And may, with one scarce less
Slight than the last, without a moment's warning
Wholly annihilate.'[8]

[8] *Poems of Leopardi* (tr. Heath-Stubbs) p. 58: from 'The Broom'.

V

CONCLUSIONS

WHAT is the moral of this essay? It is, I think, no more than this: that we should beware of feeling that scientists are (as it were) initiates, like priests; and also of contrasting the 'scientist' with the 'ordinary man' in a way in which we should never dream of contrasting the tinker or the bus-conductor with the ordinary man. For this habit is liable to weaken our critical faculty, our sense of relevance, and lead us to place too much weight on the *obiter dicta* of scientists. We should soon notice if a tinker or a bus-conductor started laying down the law about things on which his calling did not make him an authority: it is as well to bear in mind that a scientist off duty is as much an 'ordinary man' as a tinker or a bus-conductor off duty.

Once upon a time, perhaps, it would have been less easy to draw a satisfactory distinction between the explanatory and the mythological uses of our concepts. For the Ancients, there was no clear line between Atlas the astronomical notion and Atlas the mythological hero. Still, times have changed, and there is less reason nowadays for overlooking the distinctions I have been emphasizing. Like many other crucial scientific issues, the matter came to a head over the choice between the Ptolemaic and the Copernican cosmology. Until men were confronted with this choice, their own preoccupation with the Earth was reflected in the position which the Earth occupied in physical theory—the centre—so that it was possible, so to speak, to think of the importance for Man of Man's affairs as written in the skies. The result was that, when the Sun instead of the Earth was proposed as the centre of the astronomer's 'system of the world', the new theory aroused more than astronomical objections. It aroused also fear; for the picture of the Earth as being at the centre of things was, as we can now see, not only a theory but also a myth.

To begin with, the new theory was treated in a similar way. It was not felt to be enough that the mathematics of the new system were tidier than the old had been: reasons had to be found for thinking that the Sun was a *worthy* centre of things and its being the source of light and heat was argued, even by such men as Kepler, as showing that the Sun rather than the Earth was the true House of God.[1] In time, of course, people came to see that astronomical questions and questions about the ultimate importance of our mundane affairs were independent; so that their feelings of security and dignity need not remain forever tied up with problems in astronomical theory. When this happened their fear evaporated and they were happy to accept the new Copernican picture. But until it did, the myth and the theory were not clearly distinguished, and the quest for knowledge remained entangled with the quest for security.

Here, as elsewhere, we have come to distinguish between the natural sciences and other disciplines, and to disentangle from the undifferentiated skein in which they first present themselves to us the problems belonging to each. But distinctions which needed making can be forgotten again, and these particular ones are still not always clearly respected. Things which once were fused can be again confused. When we begin to look to the scientist for a tidy, a simple, and especially an all-purpose picture of the world; when we treat his tentative and carefully-qualified conclusions as universal certainties; or when we inflate some discovery having a definite, bounded scope into the Mainspring of the Universe, and try to read in the scientist's palm the solutions of difficult problems in other fields—ethics, aesthetics, politics or philosophy; then we are asking of him things he is in no position to give, and converting his conceptions into myths.

Yet how often we are liable to do this. A scientist broadcasts about his work, for instance, Fred Hoyle or Professor J. Z.

[1] Cf. S. Mason, *A History of the Sciences*, p. 144.

68

Young, and in listening to him we are always ready to find in what he tells us something more than science. What in practice we find particularly exciting, or disturbing, is not the bits of genuine science he tells us, though these are intriguing enough, so much as the philosophical or theological implications we read into them. Hoyle uses the phrase 'continuous creation' and this seizes our attention, just because it has about it a strong flavour of the Book of Genesis. Similarly, when we hear J. Z. Young talking about those 15,000,000,000 brain-cells of ours: however unjustly, we are liable to understand him, not only as suggesting what is possibly the way of working of objects whose mechanism has up to now been completely mysterious, but also as *explaining away* all kinds of things that we have hitherto had a reasoned faith in, about our minds and about our ideals.

All the same, there is no need to be bullied, or muddled, into accepting as authoritative and established scientific truths conclusions on which the scientist is in no better position to speak than anyone else. Is it suggested that perhaps our ideals are solely a question of brain-mechanism? Well, suppose that identifiable cell-structures or electronic processes were always found to be present in a man's brain if he believed, say, in freedom of speech: that would be a fascinating discovery. But even if it happened, what would it show? Need such a discovery be taken as proving anything about the importance or unimportance of our ideals? Surely not: it is not simply too soon to ask the brain physiologist questions of that sort—this is not the kind of thing he could ever be in a position to pontificate about. Brain physiology is one of the sciences which are likely to make great strides before long, but it cannot prove everything; so do not let us turn to it for guidance in problems to which it could not be relevant.

Fred Hoyle, again, is said to have composed the concluding, unscientific postscript to his book because he had been amazed at the comfort which the devout had been drawing from his first few talks. Now it was legitimate enough for him to argue that such listeners must have misunderstood his talks, and that his astrophysics could not properly be taken as bolstering up their faiths. But he seems to have felt something more than this : that, if properly understood, his theories should have been a source of positive *dis*comfort to religious people. Does this not suggest that he was deceived in the same way as they ? For what is puzzling is not people's taking comfort from an astronomical theory—seeing it as a prop for their faith—rather than having religious doubts aroused, and so feeling upset by it. What we *should* boggle at is the idea that either reaction is called for, and that any direct connection exists one way or the other between Hoyle's physics and the attitude we should adopt towards the world.

Professor Herbert Butterfield has made the point very clearly :

'When I am engaged upon a geometrical problem, or set myself to study the parts of an intricate machine, there is no reason why my mind should not try to be clear of all affections. . . . When I am thinking about man's nature and destiny, his place in the scheme of time, the posture he should adopt in the universe, and the ends that ought to be his in life, I cannot disentangle myself from my affections. Then, we make not an assertion about anything, but a decision about ourselves—we decide from what angle we will meet the stream of events and what shall be our posture as human beings under the sun.'[2]

Mutatis mutandis, Butterfield's contrast between geometry (or mechanics) and our world-views can be applied to natural science generally and, in its wider application, this contrast has been the central theme of my essay. Throughout the history of science, one finds two threads running side by side and often entangled. Much of science has always been, in Newton's phrase, 'mathematical and experimental philosophy' : many scientists, and some positivist philosophers would want to deny the name of science to any part but this. But there has in practice always been the other strand to be discerned, drawing a certain prestige lately from association with its highly successful partner—this is the strand traditionally referred to as 'natural theology'. All I have been

[2] H. Butterfield, in the *Cambridge Journal*, Vol. I, p. 8 (1948).

70

doing in this essay is applying that distinction to certain things in the science, not of the past, but of our own day.

The Creation, the Apocalypse, the Foundations of Morality, the Justification of Virtue: these are problems of perennial interest, and our contemporary scientific myths are only one more instalment in the series of attempted solutions. So next time we go into an eighteenth-century library, and notice these rows of sermons and doctrinal treatises lining the shelves, we need not be puzzled by them. Now we are in a position to recognize them for what they are: the forerunners, in more ways than one might at first suspect, of the popular science books which have displaced them.

Oxford 1951
Melbourne 1954–5

II
POETRY
AND
RELIGIOUS BELIEF

RONALD W. HEPBURN

I

INTRODUCTION

I T must be said at the outset that my contribution to this
volume consists in assembling an inventory of problems
which still await their solutions, and not in the triumphant
production of the solutions themselves. The mere setting forth
of these issues and their interrelations may, however, be worth
attempting, since the bearing of poetry upon religious belief
is far more commonly the subject of a cryptic footnote or
enigmatic final paragraph than of a sustained study—even an
exploratory one such as this. The aim of these chapters is,
then, simply to enquire into what kind of claims are being
made when someone says that certain analogies between the
language of poetry and that of religion can reduce our puzzlement over the meaning and function of religious and theological language. That is the central question: other questions
which logically are closely related to it will be discussed only
in so far as they illuminate that central target.

How, in the first place, does this group of problems arise
in actual theological argument? In many ways and in many
different situations. A theologian, for instance, may admit
to the sceptic that his theological language is logically 'odd':
'it is logically odd', he may say, 'because theology is an attempt
(an attempt we cannot avoid making) to capture the living
poetry of Scripture in the cold prose of a formal system'. Or
to the positivist, and his successors the philosophers of
language, he may say, 'I know perfectly well that my account
of religious experience is "nonsense" to the philosopher. But
it is "nonsense" in very nearly the same sense as a great deal
of poetry is "nonsense". For both involve the wresting of
words from their normal senses to allow them to say what those
normal senses can *not* say. Think of my account of religious
experience, therefore, as a stammering poetry and you won't
misunderstand it so radically nor dismiss it so hastily.'

Again, in a discussion on the justification of religious beliefs, the theologian may lead his pupil not to the arguments of rational apologetics, but instead to a work of religious poetry, which he believes is more likely to awaken faith—and to do the work of justification with less logical impropriety than the old arguments involved. It is a matter of empirical fact that through poetry such as T. S. Eliot's *Four Quartets* many people have experienced a revivifying of the ancient images, symbols and movements of thought of Christianity, which 'prose' apologetics had failed to give them.

Here, then, are two important moments of contemporary discussion in which it becomes vital to have some kind of logical map of the relation between the languages of poetry and of religion and theology. In each case we are also impelled to ask certain questions about the validity of the procedures. We want to be sure that theologians are not turning to analogies between religious language and poetry, to the study of myth and symbol and image from purely 'escapist' motives, having lost hope in the historicity of the Faith and in any evidential confirmation of the existence and nature of God. Is theology in danger (particularly in the persons of the typologists) of being transformed into a kind of literary criticism? And is the commending of religious ideas through poetry a trustworthy substitute for the discredited arguments; or could a *false* set of beliefs be mediated by a gifted poet, with equal power to convince?

Although I have no sure answer to these questions (or rather *nests* of questions), I am confident of two things; first, that the theologian's appeal to poetry can perfectly properly clarify some aspects of his use of language, if used with caution; secondly, that without such caution the appeal to poetry can easily result in a blurring of necessary distinctions and a smothering of unanswered questions. This danger is not surprising, for historically there has been about as much disagreement over the nature of the poet's use of language as over that of the theologian! Appeal from the one to the other has often come perilously near explaining *obscurum per obscurius*.

An advance summary of the five chapters of this part of

the book may help the reader to follow the direction of their argument.

II. With the typologists and other 'image'-theologians, we shall consider the Bible as a 'poem'—in the sense of being primarily a web of interlinked symbols and images. What, we shall ask, can this sort of approach show about the credibility of the Christian Faith? How far, in particular, are the sceptical implications of radical biblical criticism neutralized by discovering or re-discovering typological patterns? In what sort of way is the impressive coherence and integration displayed by the images related to the truth or falsity of the Christian claims? To justify these claims, are we in the end forced back upon cold prose?

III. Persistent religious images and patterns of images are found not only in the canonical Scriptures. Followers of Jung especially have pointed to the recurrence of similar 'archetypal images' in widely separated cultures over a great tract of time. The pressing questions here are : what *apologetic* implications follow from their persistence and from the psychologically valuable effect which is claimed when a human life is ordered round about them? and secondly, what is the logical relation between the statement 'this image constantly recurs from the remote past down to the present day' and 'this image is *of* a God who in fact exists'?

IV. To work out more fully the parallels between the languages of poetry and theology, we must undertake the analysis of some basic concepts of poetic theory—notably 'imagination', 'insight' and 'truth' (as used of a poem). It is at once obvious that the implications for a defence of Christianity are very different if we conclude with some students of poetry that poetry is 'the supreme form of emotive language' or, on the other hand, consider it quasi-mystically as a species of revelation in its own right. Are there good reasons to believe that imagination and poetic insight can give us 'news' about the nature of the world, 'reveal' to us what we have not hitherto known? or is this hint of a rapprochement between poet and prophet and Gospel-writer an illusory one? Both the language of poetry and the words of Scripture may be said to have in some sense 'transformed' or 'transfigured' the world for many of their readers. Is it chance or misleading ambiguity which permits the use of these same words 'transform' and 'transfigure' for the work of both? Or, once more, have we a genuinely illuminating analogy?

V. Poetry at its most serious and the Christian religion certainly have this in common, that both seek to integrate, to make whole, men's lives, to redeem them from bewildering 'meaninglessness', from the futility of a life seen as a patternless succession of one happening after another. In giving the symbols and structures of interpretation whereby this chaos can be exchanged for shape and articulation, do poetry and the language of religion employ similar methods? If we understand how a poem effects 'integration', are we better able to understand the corresponding impact of religious belief?

VI. Lastly: the most desirable conclusion of this comparative study would be to show that those religious uses of language which many analytic philosophers had declared meaningless were perfectly meaningful as a kind of poetry. Ordinary use would have been violated by these expressions, but only in the same sort of way as the poet or novelist (and even sometimes the scientist) violate it—in order to express what language as it stands cannot express. There can be no doubt that the religious use of many ordinary expressions is a greatly modified use; so much so that the philosopher is tempted to protest that their sense has been qualified out of existence. Perhaps the theologian could go a long way towards agreeing with the sceptic here, but suggesting that he—like the competent poet—keeps his modified senses under a strict control, a control which prevents them being altogether eroded away. I do not, however, see how to choose between these two possibilities. *Either* religious statements are semantically sound, though the words are leaning far out from their normal orbit; *or else* they maintain an *illusory* appearance of meaningfulness only. For cannot the poet too create his, highly sophisticated, forms of 'nonsense'?

II

LIVING IMAGE AND DEAD DOGMA

I. TYPES, PATTERNS AND IMAGES

If we are convinced that Hume and Kant and their successors have once and for all refuted the arguments of rational apologetics, we are faced with a choice between agnosticism (or atheism) and the discovery of an alternative method of justifying belief. Among the alternatives we may simply choose to be fools for Christ's sake, and make a frankly irrational 'leap in the dark' into faith. Or, we may develop a theology which gives supreme place, not to reason but to revelation, making the Bible our almost exclusive sourcebook instead of the cosmos at large with its 'design' or lack of design, its problems of origin and its 'contingency'. We may think of revelation as a disclosure of divine 'information'— as prose rather than poetry; or see it as working through the fabrication and development of symbols by which to interpret the nature of God and the life of man, developing in the imagination of priest and prophet under the control of the Holy Spirit. We may believe with D. D. Williams that

'today when men are more sensitive to the need for ways of expressing the meaning of life which reach beyond the literal forms of discourse, the way may be prepared for a deeper receptiveness to the Biblical conceptions. Poetry and myth . . . are forms of a more personal and concrete apprehension of truth than the plodding explications of reason can satisfactorily achieve.'[1]

A growing sense that those biblical images are the real *locus* of revelation may well be fortified by uneasiness over

[1] D. D. Williams, *Interpreting Theology 1918–1952* (SCM Press 1953), p. 35.

79

recent experiments in the 'demythologizing' of the New Testament. Many theologians protest that the translation from biblical to contemporary existentialist terms, the discarding of the biblical thought-forms as a disposable carton, loses not only the archaisms but also a good deal of the substance of revealed truth itself. 'The contents of the revelation are mysteriously inseparable from the forms in which they are conveyed'.[2] We must abandon the search after 'modern arguments for modern men', for perhaps the modern mind ought to bend back to conformity with the ancient Hebraic mind, with its concreteness, its love of intertwined type and symbol.

Theologians are still understandably perplexed by the splintering, disintegrating effect of radical biblical criticism on the conception of the Bible as single and authoritative. The question to which they are offering many different answers is 'How, if at all, can we restore our confidence in its unity? If at the textual level we find such complexity, at what level does its unity appear? At the theological level or the psychological level or where?' With Paul Tillich we may find it in the concept of the 'New Being' created under the impact of the Christ; or once again, with Lionel Thornton and Austin Farrer we may find it in the typological *liaisons*—the development throughout the corpus of Scripture of the great images—the Throne of David, the Suffering Servant, the Old Adam and the New Adam, the Old Covenant and the New Covenant. For in these patterns, rough-hewn in the Old Testament and fashioned afresh in the light of the Person of Jesus, unity and coherence are given for now and for always. There is no need, if we follow these theologians, to feel ourselves utterly at the mercy of the textual critic, who tomorrow may declare unhistorical the miracle which to-day we treasure as true. Whatever the critic says, that miracle with its symbolic material may be the vehicle of revelation, the provision of a means (the *only* means) whereby the workings of God may become known to men.

[2] L. S. Thornton, *The Common Life in the Body of Christ* (Dacre Press 1950), p. 3.

These are, I think, the main drives behind what I shall call 'the theology of images'.[3] Two additional motives may, however, be mentioned. Theologians, who believe that the importance of the Old Testament has been lately under-estimated, find in typological and related studies a means of demonstrating how little of the symbolical material of the New Testament cannot be traced back into the Old. Secondly (a motive strong in some of Farrer's recent work), New Testament writings which have been thought in the past to have a nearly haphazard arrangement can be shown by the tracing out of hitherto unnoticed patterns to have a literary shape of extraordinary symbolic complexity, in which minute details contribute to the overall plan.

2. THE THEOLOGY OF IMAGES IN ACTION

How, more precisely, does the theology of images set about its work? Primarily, as I have hinted, by tracing in the greatest detail (which we cannot here follow out) the major biblical symbol-patterns from Genesis to Revelation—or at least through as much of the Bible as they *can* be traced. The creation-images of Genesis are caught up anew in that second exhibition of divine creativity, the redemptive work of Christ: Revelation recapitulates the same thematic material (further enriched) in its vision of the new heaven and new earth. The Cross and Resurrection, as isolated events, might bewilder and mislead as much as illuminate, were it not for great archetypes like 'The Son of Man', 'the Servant', which prophet, chronicler and psalmist had wrought out of the fabric of their national life, and so furnished a fund of images by which the life of Jesus might be interpreted. It is in this sense that the Old Testament provided a 'cradle for Christ'. And it was those great interpretative images of God's relation to man which Jesus came not to destroy but to fulfil. To demythologize, therefore, or to permit the textual critic to have the last word and to sacrifice a fragment of Scripture at his behest, may be to deprive ourselves (needlessly) of links

---

[3] This nickname is a reminder that our discussion is not limited to 'typology' in the strict technical sense which some writers give the term.

in a chain of images vital for the understanding of crucial revealed truth. By being in fact *capable* of integration in a developing chain of images, a narrative, a parable, a miracle-story justifies *ipso facto* its place in the Canon. If the Scriptures were the work of a few hands writing over not very many years, this tightness of organization would still be a remarkable achievement: but when the textual critic's story is added (even a fairly *conservative* account), the unity becomes an astounding miracle. Readers of Eliot's *Four Quartets* rightly marvel that so closely organized poems could have been written over the years from 1935 to 1942: how much more remarkable, say the theologians of images, is the unity of Scripture as we discover it through typological research.

Few scholars have any objection to raise over the tracing of general image-patterns on a large canvas, such as those mentioned in my examples above. The difficulties start (and the criticism becomes strident) when the theologian claims particularly *detailed* correspondences between image and image, when he passes from the undisputable basic patterns to the more or less 'veiled' and speculative ones. For example; when Jesus told a man to stretch out his hand, and healed it, is there or is there not an echo of God's command to Moses, 'Stretch out thy hand', before Israel's deliverance from the Egyptians? Thornton says 'yes':[4] a more cautious verdict might be 'a possible echo, though not by any means a certain one'. It is no simple task to discriminate between correspondences which are the reader's creation and those which are not. Numerous criteria are relevant; sometimes none is decisive. Particularly hard to answer is the question of how complex patterns have we a right to expect in the texts before us: is it reasonable to believe that their authors *intended* this or that (often verbal and minute) liaison or allusion to earlier material? We cannot boldly answer, 'Every pattern and fragment of pattern is intended, if not by the human writer, then by the controlling Holy Spirit'; for this would plunge us back to a mechanical fundamentalism, and would foist upon the Holy Spirit any and every fanciful 'pattern' our imagina-

[4] L. S. Thornton, *The Dominion of Christ* (Dacre Press 1952), pp. 9 f.

tions succeeded in imposing on the material, however fantastic its religious implications. Criticizing his own work on Mark, Farrer writes,

'When he begins to feel qualms about the psychological credibility of what he describes, the author [i.e. himself] takes refuge in mystery, invoking the intrinsic fertility and complexity of imaginative inspiration.'[5]

To avoid this all too easy escape Farrer now admits the relevance of the author's intentions in the interpretation of what he wrote. 'An exegetical hypothesis . . . is plausible, if it can plausibly answer the question, "What did the author intend?" '[6] And this, as Farrer well realizes, is often an exceptionally hard question to answer in specific cases. Undeniably the literary tradition within which many of the New Testament writers worked relied upon typological patterning to give form to what they wrote, far more than it relied on chronological sequence. This is true even of biographical writing such as the Gospels. But it still remains problematical *to what degree of detail* a Gospel-writer articulated his book in this characteristic way, and how far, for instance, the urgency of his task dissuaded him from weaving the most minute patterns which typologists of to-day claim to find there.

Next: on what principle is the theologian to select one aspect of, say, a miracle-story for typological treatment and ignore others? Often the actual procedure here has a suspiciously arbitrary appearance. Farrer's analysis of the feedings of the thousands is based on the discovery of a numerical symbolism. But he declares that although the numbers of loaves are symbolically important, 'the fishes do not enter into the arithmetic.'[7] The wisp of justification provided for this exclusion carries little conviction.[8]

As long as attention is centred on the broad, unmistakable patterns of creation and re-creation, the old and the new

[5] Austin Farrer, *St Matthew and St Mark* (Dacre Press 1954), p. 2.
[6] *Ibid.*, p. 190.   [7] *Ibid.*, p. 65.
[8] 'Bread is the staple of the meal and a loaf is a portion. If there is some fish as well, by way of relish, so much the better; but fish do not come in standard sizes, nor is it necessary that each person's relish should be a standard amount' (*loc. cit.*).

Adam, and so on, there is little difficulty in recognizing when a particular text exemplifies or does not exemplify the image or type concerned, and it is possible to state quite adequately the theme and the links which bind certain images into a single chain. But with some groups of images the unity claimed by the typologist may be hard to verify. Is Thornton convincing, for example, in his exposition of the 'rock imagery' of the Bible in *The Dominion of Christ*? 'As the rock stopped the mouth of Sheol so Jonah stopped the mouth of the "ocean-monster".' The stone is Christ, the 'corner-stone'. Peter is also identified with it, as God may be identified with his messengers. But 'the sacred stone may be treated as a stumbling-block . . .' and so on.[9] Here the implications of the different stone-images are so diverse, even antagonistic, that only by a forced exegesis can they be thought of as *one* symbol at all. But there is no need to ridicule such attempts to push the typological approach to its limits. One cannot legislate *in advance* where the boundary between the plausible and the strained will fall. Nor can we *a priori* limit the degree of complexity in the patterns of images woven into a book of the Bible. A broad penumbra of uncertainty will probably remain between, on the one hand, undeniable concatenations of symbols and, on the other, concatenations so far-fetched that we cannot conceive them as being a serious vehicle of revelation at all, but in the spirit rather of the cross-word puzzle or the chess-problem.

Nonetheless, there *are* acrostics in the Bible, and number-symbolism which is not of our invention and often not to our taste. The importance of recalling these can be brought out in this way. If all that the theologian of images aimed to do were to make a historical study of biblical symbolism in general, then the distinction between the (to us) imaginatively impressive and the grotesquely artificial patterns would be irrelevant to his conclusions. But, although a writer like Farrer does see *part* of his work as just such a study, he also can say that the 'Evangelists' instruments were appropriate to their unique task'.[10] That is, the theologian of images tends

<hr />

[9] *The Dominion of Christ*, pp. 176 ff.   [10] *St Matthew and St Mark*, p. vii.

to claim that there is some kind of fittingness between the typological style of writing and the burden of revelation itself. This suggestion, already glanced at above, must now be examined more closely.

3. THE ORDERING OF IMAGES AND THE TRUTH OF REVELATION

Were it not for the images and their interrelations, the teaching of Jesus 'would not be supernatural revelation, but instruction in piety and morals'.[11] The stuff of inspiration is living images: to yield to these is to yield to the Holy Ghost.[12] Thus the impact of the Bible is not unlike the impact of a great poem, in which there is a constant developing and echoing of image-materials. The Book of Revelation looks back to Genesis, as the last stanza of Meredith's *Modern Love* looks back to all that has gone before. Surely the images have their own life, and the logic of their interrelation is a logic peculiar to this unique subject-matter. Here the ifs and buts of the textual critics, the inhospitable verification tests of the philosopher have become remote, scarcely audible protests.

But the position is not so simple or secure as this might suggest. In the first place, suppose we say with some theologians that the tightness of integration of theme and image in Scripture, despite its many authors living centuries apart, is itself evidence of a single Mind in command; as we might argue from the *Four Quartets* to the existence of Mr Eliot. Unfortunately, an argument like this, depending on impressions culled from a multiplicity of premisses, is desperately hard to assess. Can its main supposition be defended—the claim that we know sufficiently well the boundary between nature and supernature, between what can be done by unaided human effort and what requires divine intervention, to be sure that this growth and transformation of images could not have come about by the work of devout unaided imagination, brooding on Israel's past, and seeing that past in

11 Austin Farrer, *The Glass of Vision* (Dacre Press 1948), p. 42.
12 Austin Farrer, *A Rebirth of Images* (Dacre Press 1949), p. 18.

the light of a Jesus, who despite his stature, may not have been all the New Testament maintains?

Again, the tightness of coherence, the organic development of the images, cannot by itself bridge the gulf between aesthetic impressiveness and truth. Commentators on 'The Ancient Mariner', to take an example, have tried to show how the apparently pointless miracles described in the work are not in fact 'unmeaning marvels', but are symbolically integrated with the major themes of the poem. Now it is true that theologians of images have shown in very much the same way that the biblical miracles may be similarly integrated with the biblical themes, by finding symbolic work for *them* to do. But of course the literary critic does not want to claim that this discovery makes the story of the 'Ancient Mariner' more historically probable, nor (usually) that it makes its moral or religious meaning more acceptable. The theologian, however, seems at times to think that something of this *does* follow from his detection of close chains and patterns of biblical types and symbols. This surely will not work: for widely dissimilar tales and widely divergent 'plans of salvation' could be given *this* sort of impressiveness without ceasing to contradict one another and thus to rule out the possibility of their all being true. As a test of truth, the test of 'organic integration' is *too hospitable*. A symphony or an abstract painting may be tightly organized and yet neither true *nor* false, because 'about' nothing. Say if you like that the images combine and transform 'according to their own logic', but one must be careful not to let that force one into a position in which it becomes impossible to discriminate between the coherence of Scripture and the coherence of a nonsense poem.

So it seems that the question of the truth or falsity of what is claimed to be revelation cannot readily be established from a formal study of the 'revealed images'. Perhaps the theology of images is not self-sufficing and requires historical or other support from *outside* the circle of images. This would still be consonant with what many 'theologians of images' themselves profess. But one other line of thought may be considered briefly, which suggests that—images being what they are, and revelation coming by way of them—to step outside the circle of images is to render oneself unable to understand the subject-matter under review. A poet may say of an image in his poem, 'this image is quite untranslatable into other words: its meaning depends on the context of other images and figures in which I have set it. Give it another home outside my poem, and you give it another meaning. A paraphrase will tell a different story from the one my poem tells.' Where a poem is concerned, this plea is very often perfectly reasonable. But with a New Testament image? With an image like 'Resurrection' a somewhat different account is obviously required. The image can be traced through both Testaments in a variety of forms; and thus the language in which the Resurrection of Jesus is described cannot fully be understood in all its richness, unless the anticipations of the idea are present to the reader's imagination. If to 'translate' or 'paraphrase' here is to violate that richness, then we must not translate or paraphrase—or at least not make it a habit. But the further question still remains: is this rich complex of meaning actually applicable to the events after the death of Jesus of Nazareth? Why do we believe that this powerful image fits Jesus better than Mr X. or Mr Y.? However long we take to answer this question, we must at some stage say, 'it is because Jesus in fact rose from the dead'. This is the minimum condition for applying to him the image at all; though of course it is not the *whole* of what the image states— for the image interprets and links the bare event with before and after.

The same sort of issue may arise even for the poet or novelist. After composing the most tightly coherent sonnet to his beloved, the poet may discover that his love for her wanes and that he no longer can 'apply' the poem to her. A poem is seldom *simply* a pattern of sound and imagery without reference to any feature of the world. And in so far as a claim is made about what the world is like, that claim may turn out to be false. Shakespeare's last plays, for instance, make fascinating use of the imagery of death, quiescence and rebirth; yet a critic may say, without contradicting this, that nevertheless neither Shakespeare nor anyone else has given good reasons for believing that this pattern is to be found very often in the world we know.

It will not do then to deflect attention from the problems of historical reliability by commanding the scholar to remain within the circle of images. The 'untranslatability' of the images is one important fact about them; but another is that many of the most vital of them point beyond themselves into history. From analysing the images themselves we cannot determine whether or not we are justified in applying them to a particular historical figure or event.

In another way too we are compelled to deny the self-sufficiency of an image-theology. In *The Glass of Vision* Austin Farrer admits that it is not enough to establish a likeness between the poet and the prophet, but that important differences between their modes of inspiration must also be recognized.[13] The prophet is subject to a 'control' to which the poet is not subject. What is ultimately authoritative about the prophet's utterance is not simply and only the content of his message, but also the manner in which that message comes to him, the peculiar pressure he feels upon him. So either we describe this psychologically (and fail to find a distinction we wish to find between the prophet's state of mind and that of a wide range of abnormal conditions), or else we take *literally*—relying on their historical reliability and meaningfulness—the words with which the prophet's message is introduced in the record; 'the Word of the Lord came to the prophet X . . .'.[14] These alternatives are, no doubt, not exhaustive; but again it has become evident that study of the images themselves cannot provide a full answer to the question of the truth or falsity of an alleged revelation.

4. HISTORICITY AND THE IMAGES

As a matter of fact, both Thornton and Farrer make most generous concessions to the requirement of historicity. 'The faith of the Church [on matters such as the Resurrection]

13 Pp. 121 ff.
14 For example, see again the section of *The Glass of Vision* referred to above.

depends', Thornton writes, 'in the first instance upon questions of fact.'[15] Farrer claims that revelation takes place in the interaction between image and historical event. Here a proper stress is put upon the minimum condition of the applicability of the imagery—in our example, the actual rising of Jesus from the dead; and the image-pattern is provided for the *understanding* of what this means. But in a variety of ways these theologians (and others like-minded) show in their works that this cautious separation of event from image cannot long be maintained. The two insist on reacting upon one another—sometimes in the most puzzling fashion.

Take an example. The details of the account of John the Baptist's death parallel those of the death of Jesus with extraordinary faithfulness.[16] With a rough and approximate correspondence the reader might feel a wholesome amazement at the anticipation of the death-of-Jesus pattern within a historically reliable narrative. But where the parallels are so minute, there is a strong possibility that historicity has been sacrificed to *artificial* patterning. This is perturbing; for if revelation proceeds by the interaction of image and event, we do not wish to see the narratives which we thought recorded the hard facts being metamorphosed into structures of symbols alone. Yet, paradoxically this is one of the things that tend to happen when our typological inquiry is unusually successful, and the patterns it detects are unusually close-knit. One way out which is sometimes taken is to deny that this metamorphosis carries any sceptical implications at all. As long as the symbols concerned are consistent with our overall conception of the Christian scheme, the Person of Christ or our knowledge of God, what does it matter whether or not the narrative is fact or a symbolically 'true' fiction? This defence works well enough, *if not used too often*: for it presupposes the existence of an unchallenged core of historical belief, not itself metamorphosed to symbol: for, without this, all we should know would be symbols of symbols of symbols . . .

15 *The Common Life in the Body of Christ*, p. 257.
16 See Farrer's interesting discussion of this in *St Matthew and St Mark*, pp. 14 ff.

At any rate, the theologian who is prepared to grant the wholesale typological 'editing' of apparently narrative passages cannot afford to speak as though 'image' and 'event' were readily distinguishable in Scripture, nor to proclaim (without further *non*-imagist research) that the images may be accepted on good evidence as faithfully interpreting the events to which they claim to apply. In this respect, I think, Farrer is unduly optimistic. Confronted with the strange artifice of St Mark's number-symbolism, he writes,

'If the treasure of the Gospel has been given to us in an earthen vessel, we have to accept the fact as one further evidence that the excellency of the glory is of God and not of men.

All the divine things [Mark] wrote he deeply felt and understood for what they were, and if he chose to string them on a thread of order which was partly numerical we must be patient to follow him.'[17]

But notoriously we do not have independent access to the 'divine things' other than that which the New Testament writers themselves chose to give us, and hence no direct way of confirming the claim that Mark understood them for what they were. To the already established believer the 'earthen vessel' may stand as symbol of the glory of God. But to the sceptic, even the reluctant sceptic, language like this smoothes over abysses of uncertainty. Typological study makes him feel like a navigator of former times who learned to distrust his chart the most when it presented a coastline as a geometrically perfect ellipse or straight line. It was *too* neat to be true.

To realize that the theologian of images must work in the closest possible contact with the historical critic, and that, as we have been seeing, he cannot himself avoid playing the historical critic at certain points in his inquiry, is to be armed against the all too common belittling of historical issues in favour of an almost exclusively mythological or imagist account of Christian belief. In the work already quoted D. D. Williams describes the contemporary concern with a symbolic

17 *Ibid.*, pp. 114 f.

interpretation of 'Creation', 'the coming of the Christ, his miracles, and his resurrection from the dead, down to the assertions about final resurrection and judgment'.

'Are we dealing here [he asks] with plain "matters of fact", or rather do we not have images and symbols which express Christian convictions but which escape purely rational and factual analysis?'[18]

But in what sense do these, or some of these, images escape 'rational and factual analysis'? In the sense already discussed in which a biblical image may be 'untranslatable'—*yes*. But it may be untranslatable and yet have no application. ('Christ did not rise from the dead', for instance.) Also the list of images just quoted suggests a homogeneity among them which in fact is illusory. To distinguish the very different *sorts* of concept mentioned there, again the circle of images must be broken through. In *some* way historical research is relevant to the question of the Resurrection of Jesus in a way it is not relevant to the creation of the world and *a fortiori* to the question of its final judgment. Further, to claim that these images 'express Christian convictions' is to say that they are (among other things) appropriate vehicles for describing the events upon which this historical religion is founded. And as we have seen, such a claim cannot be argued without positing *some* non-symbolic, literal information contained in the documents about those quite 'plain matters of fact' which the images do or do not appropriately interpret. The agnostic in search of a faith may suspect once again that the best is being made of a bad job, and that he would have better reason to believe, if the Resurrection, say, did *not* thus escape factual analysis.

I have been arguing that a good deal of clarification remains to be done concerning the alleged interaction between image and event and the implications of typological detail for belief or unbelief: in the last paragraph I have added that the applicability of some images stands in need of a historical test far more than others, and that the images of the Bible cannot

18 *Interpreting Theology*, p. 34.

be treated as homogeneous, like the themes of a sonata. Both these problems are well exemplified, but not solved, in Daniélou's *Bible et Liturgie*. On the typology of the Fathers he writes,

'. . . la tradition patristique n'a fait que préciser une doctrine qui est inscrite dans les événements eux-mêmes avant de l'être dans les Écritures qui les rapportent. . . .'[19]

Patristic typology is but a continuation of biblical typology, which in turn recounts correspondences already written in historical events. Thus typology is soberly and securely anchored to *what happened*. Daniélou, however, does not seem to have linked this pronouncement with his own exegetical practice. For he takes as legitimate typological material not only what a conservative critic might accept as historically dependable, but the full range of Hebraic primitive cosmology, the ocean-monster, symbols in parables and psalms. A designer of a stained-glass window or an artist illuminating a manual of devotion might properly ignore the heterogeneity of this material. But it is quite another matter when a theologian professes that his types bear a close relation to historical fact. In *this* case the work of discrimination and the relating of symbol to event cannot be shunned.

The theologian of images is faced with two problems, the one tractable, the other most intractable. The first is the problem of presenting to the twentieth century reader the *meaning* of biblical concepts; to recreate for him their complex liaisons throughout the enormous corpus of Canonical and sometimes also non-Canonical literature. This task is very close to that of a literary critic like Caroline Spurgeon in her work on Shakespeare's imagery—providing the reader with the full weight of meaning the author put into his writing. Here the biblical theologian has been markedly successful. The second problem is not of meaning but of *reference*: do these images apply to the world as it is in fact? Here his voice is much less authoritative, his study is no

---

[19] Jean Daniélou, S.J., *Bible et Liturgie* (Paris 1951), p. 239.

longer autonomous. Indeed, some of his brightest successes in the first task seem to thwart the successful advancement of the second—as when historically vital sources display patterns 'too good to be true'. Or if he sees no threat here, he must at least back up in a detailed (non-typological) way his continued trust that his symbols rest on a firm historical substratum.

III

ARCHETYPE AND MYTH

None of the criticisms of the image-theology made in the preceding pages has sought to discredit the importance of the great biblical types and symbols for any theory of revelation. I have claimed no more than the insufficiency of a study of these to answer *by itself* the question of the truth or falsity of a historical revelation. Someone might argue, however, that half the story remains untold so long as the scrutiny is confined to the Bible itself. For we find even in widely separated cultures at quite different epochs remarkably similar religious images spontaneously arising in the human mind. Certain symbols of deity, instruments of meditation like the 'mandala' diagram, patterns of death and return to life—are the monopoly of no single cult, no single sacred volume. The question immediately re-asserts itself, do we need to insist, as I have been insisting, upon minute historical confirmation of events or a particular time and place, when we are furnished with such a cloud of symbolic witness to the hardiness of religious belief? Documentary anxieties seem pointless quibbles, if in the unconscious mind of every man are imprinted these basic images. If, say, Jung's account of the 'collective unconscious' can be followed, then we have in its 'archetypes' a wonderful proliferation of manuscript authority and a most accessible one!

As is well known, Jung refuses to see the unconscious simply as a repository for repressed infantile, mainly sexual, memories. In his view it contains more than can be accounted for in terms of the individual's actual experience. Agnostics of our own day, for instance, dream the religious symbols of cults they 'know' nothing of. The peculiar sense of authority and 'otherness' which accompany those archetypal images testifies to their mysterious source.

Two lines of thought immediately demand to be explored. Is the occurrence of the archetype 'God' any evidence at all for the actual *existence* of God? Does the 'imprint' of the type entail an 'Imprinter'? Secondly, what are we to make of Jung's claim that 'the archetypes of the unconscious can be shown empirically to be the equivalents of religious dogmas'?[1] Many people superficially acquainted with the Jungian approach have concluded from a statement like this that problems of historical confirmation and philosophical anxieties over meaning can be circumvented by such 'empirical' psychological discovery. Are they justified in their confidence? If I entertain the image, and dwell upon it, *am* I accepting the religious dogma 'equivalent' to it? If so, we should have arrived by a new route at a truly self-sufficient theology of images.

But in each case disappointing qualifications must at once be made. The presence of the archetypes is just one more brute fact which the psychologist describes more or less reliably. Jung has denied (at least in some of his books) that he has any warrant to pass from the recognition of this fact to the claim, 'objects exist corresponding to the images' : they are not self-authenticating. Although we may speak of an imprint, we have no more authority than before to posit an Imprinter. In the second case the indefiniteness of the archetypes, their openness to numerous interpretations from the viewpoints of incompatible faiths, makes them unsatisfactory instruments for certifying any one religion as true; and as in the case of the divine archetype itself the appearance of the images supplies no warrant to posit the objectivity of what they seem to tell us.

Why then, if these qualifications are so formidable and can be so quickly stated, has the Jungian account of archetypes made the impact it has made? And how do intelligent people continue to see in it apologetic possibilities? The

[1] C. G. Jung, *Psychology and Alchemy* (Routledge and Kegan Paul 1953), p. 17.

reasons, I think, are of several different sorts. One of the most important is the slipperiness of the Jungian vocabulary, its use of picturesque metaphors which easily suggest misleading implications.

(i) Even if no claim is made about an Imprinter, the language of 'print', 'stamp' is constantly on the point of begging the question; since in almost every other context 'print' *does* entail 'printer'. In a similar way 'design' normally entails 'designer'—a fact crucial to the criticism of the traditional 'argument from design' to the existence of God. Just as one should avoid the language of 'print' until we are prepared to postulate a printer, so the orderliness found in nature should not be named 'design' until it seems to demand a designer. The real crux of the arguments is not the transition from 'print' to 'printer' or 'design' to 'designer' (for these are nearly *analytically* true), but the decision that the language of 'print' or 'design'—with all its implications—is the most appropriate one.

(ii) Jung and Jungians employ a remarkable range of analogies in their accounts of the collective unconscious and its archetypes. In one context the archetypes are thought of as deposits from the remote past of human racial experience, traces which doubtless have their physiological basis in inherited features of brain structure. On the other hand, we also read in dramatic metaphor of 'invasions' from the collective unconscious, a figure which *externalizes* the unconscious, and suggests strongly that we are 'visited' from something not ourselves when the archetypes are present to us. From this the transition to revelation language (or at least to the 'divine Imprinter') is easy. In his *Answer to Job* Jung uses an even bolder manner of speech, which he does not satisfactorily relate to the less pretentious metaphors from which he starts:

'. . . the archetypes of the collective unconscious . . . precipitate complexes of ideas in the form of mythological motifs. Ideas of this kind are never invented, but enter the field of inner perception as finished products, for instance in dreams. They are spontaneous phenomena which are not subject to our will, and we are *therefore* [my italics] justified in ascribing to them a certain autonomy. . . . [they are] subjects with laws of their own . . . they possess spontaneity and purposiveness, or a kind of consciousness and free will.'[2]

Here in a very few words we can see an illicit transition from the denial of conscious control over the archetypes to the philosophically misleading personification of them as conscious beings existing over-against the subject concerned! Metaphor has taken over the work of argument.

(iii) Research into the collective unconscious, Jung believes, has made it clear as never before that man has a 'natural religious function'. Deprive him of its exercise and his mental health is disturbed. This again seems to be empirical confirmation of at least *some* of the Christian's claims. If it can be accepted, then the very presence of the images and their empirical effects on those who entertain them may yield proof of what the philosopher of religion and the biblical critic have sought, but so often failed to demonstrate.

Unfortunately, both 'natural' and 'function' are notoriously treacherous words with so many levels of ambiguity, that it is not at all clear what is being asserted in this context. The most usual 'home' of the phrase 'natural function' is probably a physiological one—the functions of sleep, digestion and so on. These can be discussed in terms of needs and the satisfaction of needs. By analogy then men have religious needs and, by way of the archetypes, the means of satisfying them. This, so far, is a possible way of speaking, but very quickly the analogy breaks down. We could not withhold the name 'food' to what relieved hunger and provided nourishment to the body, but it might be argued that we are *not* similarly entitled to call whatever administers religious peace of mind, or excites reverence or praise, an independently existing 'God'. A logical wedge can be inserted in the religious case, which cannot in the case of 'food'; namely, the question, Have I correctly *interpreted* the images and their psychological impact upon me—as pointing to a Being beyond themselves? The

[2] C. G. Jung, *Answer to Job* (Routledge and Kegan Paul 1954), pp. xv f.

language of 'natural function' blurs over this crucial question; suggests that it need not arise. This point will shortly be elaborated further.

If the Jungian is too eager sometimes to describe religious notions in pseudo-scientific terms, he is equally prone to attempt also the opposite—to incorporate religious concepts within psychological descriptions in a way that again arouses misleading expectations. Jung narrates a vision, which had a profoundly therapeutic effect upon one of his patients.[3] It seemed to be 'an attempt to make a meaningful whole from . . . formerly fragmentary symbols', archetypal in origin. 'The vision', says Jung, 'was a turning point in the patient's psychological development. It was what one would call—in the language of religion—*a conversion.*'[4] One cannot read such an account without being tempted to conclude that the language of 'conversion' has been shorn of some of its theological perplexity. But how far is this true? Can we make sense of 'conversion' in its religious contexts in terms of a gain in psychological stability through an archetypal vision, as we might call it? Not to any great extent. For to be converted in the Christian sense is not simply to see visions or dream dreams or even to be restored and elevated by such, but also to be prepared to make certain 'existential' claims—that *God is*, that Jesus of Nazareth was his Son, that he shall come to judge the quick and the dead . . . 'Conversion' admittedly means far more than 'being convinced of the truth of . . .'. It entails commitment and a practical reorientation of life. But 'being convinced of the truth' is still an *essential* element in the complex. Jung may use the word 'conversion' in that weak sense which *excludes* the element of conviction, or leaves the question of conviction open. But used without qualification the expression is very likely to convince the reader that more has been done towards relieving the Christian problem of conversion of its intricacy than has been done in fact.

[3] C. G. Jung, *Psychology and Religion* (New Haven; Yale University Press 1938), pp. 79 ff.
[4] *Ibid.*, p. 80, italics mine.

2. HISTORICAL PERSISTENCE AND THERAPEUTIC POWER

Lack of linguistic caution is not, however, the only or the chief difficulty in assessing the 'argument from archetype'. Two aspects require especial attention, the historical persistence of the archetypes and their therapeutic power.

(i) By contemplating the procession of the images from culture to culture, century to century, one may readily come to feel that particular recent problems of meaning and historical confirmation are of little moment, that no challenge at the level of rational argument can shake or oust so permanent a feature of human experience. We feel about this testimony what T. S. Eliot feels about 'the mind of Europe', in relation to the poet—'a mind which he learns in time to be much more important than his own private mind'.[5] But where the archetypes are concerned, two difficulties stand in the way. First, there is no *logical* ground for equating the long-lasting with the 'divine', despite Platonic temptations. There is no contradiction in saying 'X has existed as long as mankind' and also that X is false or bad, or has been wrongly interpreted. Second, if the Jungian account of the origin of the collective unconscious is acceptable, then what we there encounter is the deposit not of human experience at its most acute and informed but at its most primitive and untutored. No good reason has been given for looking on this deposit as more likely than contemporary experience and reflection to be adequate to the facts about the world. In what way did primitive man have privileged access to those truths which are now incapsulated symbolically in our unconscious? Once more, the images themselves cannot reveal to us the grounds of their possible authoritativeness.

(ii) In *Psychology and Religion* Jung asks, 'Is there, as a matter of fact, any better truth about ultimate things than the one that helps you to live?'[6] Cannot the questions of theologians and metaphysicians be by-passed in the interest

---

[5] T. S. Eliot, *Tradition and the Individual Talent.*
[6] *Psychology and Religion*, pp. 113 ff.

of a pragmatic test of religious truth, such as this? The doubts expressed above on the idea of religion as a 'natural function' are relevant here; but more needs to be said. Jung's suggestion is that we in fact have no independent access to 'ultimate things': we can only see the effect of archetypal contemplation on the believer or sceptic. And this suffices.

'A thing that cures a neurosis must be as convincing as the neurosis; and since the latter is only too real, the helpful experience must be of equal reality. It must be a very real illusion, if you want to put it pessimistically. *But what is the difference between a real illusion and a healing religious experience?* It is merely a difference in words.'[7]

The pessimist, he goes on, may define life as 'a disease with a very bad prognosis'; this is simply to render the word 'disease' meaningless (save for its unpleasant emotive overtone) by extending its scope to cover even its opposite—'health'. Is Jung right in asserting that to call a therapeutically effective 'religious experience' illusory is a comparable piece of word-juggling? No: the man who said 'the religious experience was indeed therapeutic, but still illusory' need not be pointlessly extending the concept of illusion. He may wish (with complete logical propriety) to question the patient's *interpretation* of what he experienced, to deny that his experience was 'of' an existent God, that it possessed cognitive content, that it gave any grounds of confidence, say, in a life hereafter. And such objections, even if neither verifiable nor falsifiable, are meaningful, and his use of 'illusory' is meaningful, despite Jung's embargo.

The movement of thought behind this appeal to the therapeutic power of the images might be expressed as follows: 'all we know of "ultimate truth" is what is implied by those conceptions which minister to human wellbeing, in particular by means of the archetypes mediating experiences that make life "healthier, more beautiful, more complete and more satisfactory".'[8] But this statement is logically obscure. It

[7] *Ibid.*, *loc. cit.*, italics mine.　　　　[8] *Ibid.*, p. 114.

hovers between being 'analytic'—true through our agreement
to use words in a particular way, and 'synthetic'—true as a
piece of reliable news about the world. Part of the difficulty in
knowing how to handle it, how to confirm or reject it, comes
from just this ambiguity of form. It is analytic if 'ultimately
true' is *defined* in terms of therapeutic efficacy. 'We shall call
"ultimately true" whatever in fact leads to "beauty, com-
pleteness . . ." and the rest.' It is synthetic if we mean that
conceptions which minister to human wellbeing are most
likely as a matter of fact to be true—in a *non*-pragmatic sense
of 'true'. The analytic version of course needs no evidential
support; but there is much to be said against its definition of
truth, although that question cannot be pursued here. The
synthetic version is plainly in need of a *great deal* of evidential
backing. Why should we believe the world to be so hospitable
to humanity as this view demands? Demonstration here is
likely to be hard, for theological concepts (which the argument
is aimed finally at justifying) cannot be used to support the
argumentation which seeks to establish them: or else the
entire procedure will be circular. The psychologist or
philosopher who makes the appeal to therapy, if he is not on
guard, fails to see that he is committed to this demonstration
at all; for the *analytic* interpretation (not clearly recognized
as such) is at hand to lull him to a false security, through its
suggestion of self-evidence.

3. MARSHALLING THE IMAGES: PROBLEMS OF THEIR AMBIVALENCE

Earlier in this chapter I took notice of the indifference of
the archetypes to specific religious dogmas: where these latter
disagree, the images cannot usually further the task of discrimination between them. The archetype of the 'divine birth'
cannot answer the question *which* claimant to divinity is
authentic and which is not. Still more troubling, the image of
the 'hero' is manifested in the Nazi mythos as patently as in
the Christian. The archetypes are present in Dante's *Divina
Commedia*, in Blake, Kafka and Yeats; and how very different
are the things they say, how many voices they have. Speaking

in the most general terms, the sense of momentousness carried by the archetypes, their combination of aesthetic and numinous power, their wide symbolizing capacity, do not guarantee ethical and religious unanimity among those who employ them. They have their diabolical as well as their benign interpretation—as when a Fascist airman machine-gunning a crowd of civilians saw their rush to escape under the simile of an expanding, opening rose. Myths *may* be the 'fundamental expressions of human nature' as Jung holds; but the grandiose suggestions of 'fundamental' must not be taken to assert that from the myths and the archetypes we can *read off* a pattern for human life. Rather, the ambivalent archetypal material stands in need of a moral control, which itself is not 'given' with the material. The authority of the images is not complete; they must be marshalled according to laws of which they know nothing.

But to what extent *are* the reins in our hands? If we were simply devising a rhapsody of images, constructing a myth at once morally noble and psychologically valuable, we should have no difficulty once we had found empirically *which* images did this satisfactorily, and had arrived at a way of combining them elegantly. But this is so unlike any serious account of how men attain knowledge of religious truth, so completely replaces humility under revelation by initiative in the manipulation of images whose source is unknown, that something must have gone drastically wrong with our analysis, if this conclusion seems forced on us. The suspicion is most dramatically confirmed by Jung's essay, *Answer to Job*.

The problem from which this book starts is Jahweh's 'immoral' treatment of Job. Job's agony is connived at by Yahweh: Satan and he are practically collaborators in experimenting on Job's loyalty. Job does not even receive an intelligible account of why he must suffer; he is simply treated to a demonstration of Yahweh's might. God must now, says Jung, make amends for this appalling immorality.

'That is why Sophia steps in. She reinforces [Yahweh's] much needed self-reflection and thus makes possible Yahweh's decision to become man . . . he raises himself above his earlier primitive level of consciousness by indirectly acknowledging that the man Job is morally superior to him and that therefore he has to catch up and become human himself.'[9]

Sophia, the divine principle of wisdom, corresponds to the female element in the godhead, recognized in numerous religions from the most remote past. 'Even in prehistoric times' it was realized 'that the primordial divine being is both male and female'.[10] Without such a female element no conception of God is complete, and no worshipper of such a God can be wholly at peace. The religion of Old and New Testaments is psychologically sound only if Sophia's importance is seen in the Old and that of the equivalent figure of the Virgin Mary in the New. Jung's stress on the moral inadequacy of Yahweh and his need to atone leads him to acclaim enthusiastically the Dogma of the Bodily Assumption of Mary, a long-due recognition of the feminine, reconciling aspect of God. The Protestant failure to sympathize with this dogma is only one symptom of its general refusal to give 'the archetypal symbolisms the necessary freedom and space in which to develop over the centuries'.[11]

Here quite plainly the selection and solemnizing of images is carried out on principles far different from those of dogmatic theology or historical research as ordinarily conceived. Jung has the reins firmly in his hands, as he fashions a psychologically and morally acceptable creed out of the archetypal material found in Scripture and the contemporary mind. How does he try to justify his procedure?

First, by asserting a sharp dichotomy between 'physical fact' and 'psychic truth'. The flotilla of images is not to be moored by chains of historical credibility! To obtain agreement, for example, about the Virgin Birth, all that needs to be done is to renounce the pointless habit of thinking of this as a 'physical fact'.[12] 'Beliefs of this kind are psychic facts which cannot be contested and need no proof.' Nor does it

[9] *Answer to Job*, p. 69. [10] *Ibid.*, p. 166.
[11] *Ibid.*, p. 172. [12] *Ibid.*, p. xi.

matter that dogmas describe the physically impossible; why *should* the logic of the archetypes conform to rational discourse about the observable world?[13]

Secondly, taking this last point further, theologians and philosophers of religion should not be afraid of the paradoxical, have no reason whatever for seeing it as an offence to the coherence and intelligibility they desire. However difficult it may be to describe the status of Mary in heaven, 'at any rate her position satisfies the need of the archetype';[14] and that is enough. God, Jung claims, can be conceived as 'an eternally flowing current of vital energy . . . just as easily as we can imagine him as an eternally unmoved, unchangeable essence'.[15] Yes, indeed; or equally easily in a great variety of other ways, if we avail ourselves of Jung's unlimited freedom of paradox and contradiction. This is our uneasiness; we have lost the sense of that characteristic theological tension—between the ordinary use of words and their religious employment, a tension without which a theology has no guard against extravagance and nonsense disguised as super-sense.

But it can readily be seen how with these principles of method Jung feels justified in creating his free-fantasy upon biblical theology. What is more, he attempts to do this and yet to pay lip-service to Christianity as a historical religion, the doctrines of which are subject to the challenge, 'Did this happen in history?' and the language of which is not always the paradoxical language of the archetypes but also the prosaic language of 'Now it came to pass . . .' How can Jung, without re-introducing the theological tensions he has renounced, accommodate both the literal 'He was brought up in Nazareth' with the dogmatic 'He is very God of very God'? His attempt takes the following shape.

(i) Very little knowledge can be claimed of the details of Jesus' historical life.

(ii) Yet even if his life-story were a myth, that would not be to call it fiction; for the myth draws attention to constantly repeated facts and patterns of existence. The archetypes ful-

---

[13] *Ibid.*, pp. xii ff.   [14] *Ibid.*, p. 171.   [15] *Ibid.*, p. xiii.

filled themselves in the life of Jesus—hence the universal relevance of his life.

Two protests need to be made here. One: that such an account does scant justice to the Christian belief of the absolutely *un*repeatable nature of the Incarnation. Two: to say that myth is concerned with '*facts* that are continually repeated and can be observed over and over again',[16] blurs the gap between the historical 'factual' claims of Jesus' biographers—that he healed the sick and rose from the dead, and on the other hand the 'psychic facts' which repeat themselves whenever this or that archetype rules a person's life. Apart from an undeveloped hint that 'objective, non-psychic parallel phenomena can occur which also represent the archetype',[17] it is the latter psychic facts with which Jung concerns himself throughout. Jung's language suggests that nothing is lost in the transition from historical truth to mythological truth. But the Christian position is very different, insisting, as it does, that the mythological, psychic importance of Jesus' life springs from certain events of that life which occurred in the most brutely factual manner, involving nails and a cross and an empty tomb.

(iii) In the preceding chapter I tried to show that a typologist who exaggerated the self-sufficiency of his method tended to ignore vital differences of status among his image-materials. Jung faces a similar problem due to his supreme concern with manifestations of the archetypes and his near-indifference to history. It is difficult, for instance, to discover from *Answer to Job* what ontological difference, if any, exists between Lilith, Job, Sophia and the Virgin Mary. And yet if we do not attach supreme importance to this question, nothing stands in the way of each man constructing his own faith after his own heart's desires, bound to psychologically satisfying archetypes and to nothing besides.

The reader may have been feeling that some of these Jungian notions have been too extravagant to merit serious discussion. They have been considered here, however, as illuminating examples of what happens when a theology of

---

[16] *Ibid.*, p. 75.　　　　[17] *Ibid.*, p. 76.

images tries to become really autonomous and at the same time to remain hospitable to Christian orthodoxy. Critics of theologians like Austin Farrer and Lionel Thornton have feared (over-anxiously) that they were moving towards just such dangers in teaching that the image and pattern were the primary vehicles of revelation. But they have refused (save for occasional lapses) to release the tensions, as the Jungians release them, between the images and history, and between the 'logic of the images' and the logics of ordinary discourse. These tensions cannot be relaxed without disaster. Nor can the theologian confidently manipulate the images into therapeutically effective patterns, not at least while also claiming to interpret a revelation of which mankind is the humble *recipient*.

4. SYMBOLS CREATED AND SYMBOLS RECEIVED

Before ending this chapter, something more needs to be said on the problem mentioned in the last sentence and elsewhere. My general worry about Jung's procedure was that he seems to exchange the crucial idea of *receptivity* under divine revelation for human *activity* in the marshalling of the archetypes. At the same time we did notice Jung's own account of where receptivity is inescapable—namely, in sitting under the archetypes themselves, which are not wholly at the beck and call of consciousness, and are taken by him as having a strange autonomy of their own. There is a dilemma here, which points again to the unanswered question—'Whence do the images derive their authoritativeness in the first place?' The arguments from historical persistence and from therapeutic power we had reason to distrust: there remains the peculiar impact of the images themselves, their characteristic 'otherness', which strikes us quite differently from our normal memories of the past and seems to refer to no product of human inventiveness. It is this feature of their impact which gives plausibility to the metaphor of 'invasion' from the collective unconscious and to the claim that to encounter the archetypes is to come as near as we ever can to an encounter with 'ultimate truth'.

Now, revelation may well come by way of the images: but even admitting that, it is exceptionally hard to exclude alternative hypotheses about their origin which carry very different implications. The Freudians have shown, on the one hand, how experiences of very early childhood may present themselves to the adult as remote, 'other-worldly' in tone, not continuous with more accessible memories but rather like an intrusion from altogether outside our experience; and on the other hand many basic human *artefacts* such as language tend to acquire the tone of something received as a gift of grace—'given', not 'made'. Ernst Cassirer describes this in his essay, *Language and Myth*:

'. . . while logical reflection tends . . . to resolve all receptivity into spontaneity [as when we discover the activity of the mind in knowing], mythic conception shows exactly the opposite tendency, namely to regard all spontaneous action as receptive and all human achievement as something merely bestowed.'[18]

Were the archetypes an ultimately man-made instrument for externalizing or at least symbolizing human conflicts and aspirations, they might still come with the same sense of otherness and the same claims to 'authority'. Maybe they are *not* artefacts; but the archetypal theory which we have discussed above is clearly not sufficiently well-founded nor well-defended against such alternatives that it can afford to pay them no heed.

Finally, what I have just said, following Cassirer, about the difficulty sometimes met in distinguishing the 'given' from the 'made', is relevant in more than one way to this study as a whole. For part of what we mean by calling a *poem* 'authoritative', or claiming for it a 'visionary' grandeur, is precisely that we do not feel in the presence of a laboured artefact when reading it, although we may know that it was the product of the greatest labour, but in the presence of something inevitable, waiting 'out there' to be discovered by the poet, who seems more amanuensis than creator. All I wish to

[18] Ernst Cassirer, *Language and Myth* (New York 1946), p. 60.

conclude at this stage is that the sense of 'givenness'—of an archetype or of a poem—is not an infallible one, and the former cannot be reliably taken as the foundation of an account of revelation through the image, any more than the latter entails that the poet is secretary to a dictating Muse.

IV

INSIGHT AND IMAGINATION

So far we have been trying to explore the possibilities of a theology which attempts to side-step unmanageable problems of meaning and reference by considering the image, type or symbol as the vehicle of revelation, instead of the proposition. Our conclusion has been that the attempt produces valuable insights but does not possess the self-sufficiency sometimes claimed for it. Questions of historical reference, in particular, cannot be eliminated, and I shall also show in a later chapter that a theology of images does not really escape many of those problems of meaning which the philosopher of language has detected in the 'prose' discourse of theology.

Our task in this section, however, is to clarify the Analogy which we have uncritically been assuming throughout— the Analogy between the religious type or image and the poetic image.[1] If we say the image in Scripture is the all-important thing, that the prophet's inspiration is not altogether unlike the poet's, that the languages both of religion and of poetry make meaningful use of what in prose is properly labelled nonsense, that the poet's 'insight' and 'imagination' have their close parallels in the literary work of a St Mark or St Paul, then we imperatively need to know how the poet uses language, what the poet's 'inspiration' is like, what kind of 'insight' and 'imagination' he manifests. Widely different answers are possible in the case of the poet; and thus equally widely different analogous conclusions about the writers of Scripture and their revealed images. To start with two extreme views:

[1] For brevity, I shall refer to this as 'the Analogy' with a capital 'A'.

(i) The poetic image, someone might say, tells us nothing whatever about our world (or any other world). Its function is not to describe but to express and evoke emotion. If the Analogy is sound, revelation similarly can give us no news, bears no cognitive content, works only upon our feelings.

(ii) In very different vein, someone else may say, The poet is an explorer who glimpses what normally is beyond human sight. He is at the same time passive under an inspiration which he cannot command at will. He does not so much *speak* as allow himself *to be spoken through*. The prophet likewise is a discoverer of the truth inaccessible to his unaided effort. The Analogy illuminates the prophet's work and ennobles the poet's.

I think it can be shown that neither of these extreme views —the sceptical or the reverential shortcut—survives much scrutiny.

I. WHY THE 'EMOTIVE' ACCOUNT FAILS

Logical Positivism, which gave rise to the 'emotive' analyses of poetry, distinguished three basic functions of language. Language could *describe* the world as the scientist describes it: whatever is truly asserted may be experimentally confirmed. Language may also be used, not to give information, but to state the relations between our agreed use of symbols, as in the formula $(a - b)^2 = a^2 - 2ab + b^2$. Or, thirdly, it may not *state*, but express or evoke feeling, perhaps while *seeming* (misleadingly) to state fact of some kind. Since the poet is in competition neither with the scientist nor with the mathematician, it seemed reasonable to classify his utterances as emotive; the poetic image was a pseudo-statement, whose real job was not stating anything at all. No detailed analysis of poetic language was ever worked out *solely* in terms of emotive impact. The early work of I. A. Richards, although it declared poetry to be 'the supreme form of emotive language',[2] found it necessary to speak also of the evocation of 'attitudes' which cannot be analysed in terms of emotion alone. And in the last

[2] I. A. Richards, *Principles of Literary Criticism* (Routledge and Kegan Paul 1949: first published 1924), p. 273.

few decades philosophers have been compelled to reject the threefold analysis of language-functions, as more and more quite distinct uses have been identified. One important recent addition is the 'performatory' use, language as *intervention in the world*, as when I utter the words 'I promise', 'I approve', 'I baptize'. Here nothing is being described (save indirectly), nor is my aim the arousing of emotion. But after my words have been spoken, the situation in which I find myself has been changed—by the very uttering of the words themselves.

Now, the emotions 'attached' to words are certainly more relevant to the poet's use of them than normally to the scientist's. Compare the word 'star' in an astronomical learned journal and in the sonnet beginning 'Bright star! would I were steadfast as thou art . . .' But with the discovery of *numerous* linguistic functions until recently neglected, the philosopher is no longer tempted to say that a poet need be concerned only with that emotive meaning. The poet may, in addition, state resemblances between elements of his experience, coax his reader into seeing X 'in the light of' Y, help him to reorganize his 'slant' on the world. Indeed, to say that the poet seeks to communicate 'feelings' is not necessarily to claim that he aims above all to impart *emotions*: he may 'feel *that*' A is like B or *that* M can be understood afresh if seen from the standpoint of N. Here 'feeling that' is equivalent to 'suspecting that', 'having a good idea that', and cannot be assimilated to 'having an emotion'.[3]

In view of all this, it does not seem inevitable that if we posit a close analogy between the language of poetry and that of religion we are necessarily committed to analysing both in terms of 'emotive meaning' and thus making nonsense of any cognitive claims either may make.

2. 'INSPIRATION' AND POETIC WORTH

To say that a poet is under 'inspiration' is *prima facie* to make a psychological judgment and not simply a logical or aesthetic

[3] See Gilbert Ryle, 'Feelings', in *Aesthetics and Language* (Blackwell 1954), pp. 56 ff. On this theme see also William Empson, *The Structure of Complex Words*, especially the early chapters.

one. We seem to be saying something about the condition of his psyche at the time of composition, or just before composition starts. But the study on which we are engaged is primarily a logical comparison of the languages of poetry and religion, and psychological issues are relevant to it only where these may have logical implications. One such case was mentioned in Chapter III when we noted the tendency to see certain human artefacts as passively received gifts—a psychological fact which might well have to be 'allowed off' in coping with the peculiarly slippery logic involved in the description of archetypes. That 'inspiration' also has a bearing on logical as well as psychological inquiry can be brought out in this way.

Suppose that two writers experience what they claim to be inspiration. Their descriptions of their experiences tally in all relevant respects, but the poems which result are of very different value. We may wish to say that the one writer was truly inspired and that the other only seemed to be. But from this it is obvious that the written poem and a critical assessment of it are relevant to answering the question 'Was it inspiration?' as much as a report of how the poet felt at the time of composition. In fact, *more* relevant: for a critic may unhesitatingly call a poem 'inspired' although he has seen nothing but the lines on the page and has no knowledge whatever of its author or of his state of mind when he wrote it. In short, the bogus and the true in inspiration may be indistinguishable at the psychological level, but perfectly distinguishable at the level of the written poem. To enquire into the success or failure of a poem, into what it communicates and how, no excursus into the poet's biography is required. Now what follows from all this for the Analogy which is our principal concern, that between the poem and the revealed image? It serves to make us cautious of the argument that to know what it is for a poem to be 'inspired' is to be already half-way to granting the intelligibility of the *prophet's* 'inspiration' also, of his receptivity to the divine oracle. For to call the author of a canonical book 'inspired' *is* to say something about more than the prophecy he has uttered or the Gospel he has written. It *is* to describe the circumstances of its composition, the origin of its material; and here the Analogy with the inspiration of the poet is at its weakest. Since 'inspiration' is used by the critic as a general term of strong commendation, its logic is too far removed from that of religious 'inspiration' to provide a secure stepping-stone to understanding and assessing the sacred authors' claims.

Both these shortcuts fail. The Analogy between poetic and religious uses of language does not entail that both are emotive and non-cognitive : and to call a poet 'inspired' is not to credit him with a prophet-like access to esoteric truth. Nothing I have said of course *denies* that the poet may have such access; only, the common language of inspiration is not by itself enough to demonstrate it. A more sober and painstaking enquiry into the poet's activity might reveal more accurately what degree of rapprochement there is between him and the prophet. The notions of 'imagination', 'insight' and 'truth' might be crucial to this exploration. To these we shall now turn.

3. IMAGINATION, INSIGHT AND TRUTH

The three concepts are almost inextricably intertwined in some forms of poetical theory. Basil Willey, for instance, in his essay on Coleridge, states that the Coleridgean distinction between 'imagination' and 'fancy' deepens our understanding of questions like 'Is poetry an approach to *truth*?'[4] Keats declared that 'the Imagination may be compared to Adam's Dream—he awoke and found it truth' and 'what the imagination seizes as Beauty must be truth'.[5] Similar lofty cognitive claims are made in J. Middleton Murry's *Discoveries*. Some poetry

'is the direct embodiment, through symbols which are necessarily dark, of a pure, comprehensive and self-satisfying experience, which we may call, if we please, an immediate intuition into the hidden nature of things.'[6]

4. Basil Willey, *Nineteenth Century Studies* (Chatto and Windus 1950), p. 11.
5 John Keats, *Letters*, ed. M. B. Forman, No. 31.
6 J. Middleton Murry, *Discoveries* (Jonathan Cape 1930), p. 42.

If language like this should give a faithful and economical account of poetic communication, if every time we pronounced a serious poem 'imaginative' we should be committed (to avoid self-contradiction) to those theories of imagination as truth-achieving, then our Analogy should be enormously reinforced, and what we did not manage to establish by study of modes of inspiration should be equally soundly established through analysis of *imagination*. If, on the contrary, these accounts should prove to be uneconomical, 'inflated', solemn rhetoric rather than cool description, then our experiment in thinking of the revealed image as a kind of poetry would be less illuminating than we should have liked.

Coleridge thinks of the imagination in two contrasted ways. These ways may perhaps combine in his thought into a single view, as I. A. Richards for one believes. I shall not, however, argue this question, since the two views provide in themselves a convenient expository framework for our study, and Coleridgean exegesis is not our aim. Imagination, then, is seen as creative and as cognitive; it makes and it discovers truth, often truth about the half-seen familiar.

(i) Imagination as creative. This view does have theological implications, but they are not relevant to our primary task. 'Art', says Maritain, 'is not a caricature of creation, it *continues* creation'.[7] The writer or artist who believes this imparts to his art a sacramental solemnity. But first he must *already* understand the expression 'divine creation' and must have satisfied himself that the expression has reference as well as meaning. What we are seeking at the moment is help through the Analogy, in understanding the *meaning* of theological concepts: whereas in this instance such understanding is presupposed.

(ii) The imagination discovers, apprehends. In Eliot's words:

'I may say that the great poet . . . should perceive vibrations beyond the range of ordinary men, and be able to make men see

[7] Jacques Maritain, *Art and Poetry* (PL Editions Poetry 1945), p. 30.

and hear more . . . than they could ever see or hear without his help.'[8]

He is an 'explorer beyond the frontiers of ordinary consciousness' who seeks to 'return and report to his fellow-citizens'; and so on.

It is tempting for the hard-headed philosopher of language to dismiss this conception of imagination as simply in conflict with the ordinary use of the words 'imagine' and 'imaginary'. Thus the late Margaret MacDonald in an Aristotelian Society paper:

'Imagining and creating may be successful or unsuccessful ("I tried to imagine a battlefield, but failed"; "I tried to write a novel but found it impossible"), but cannot as such be right or wrong, inform or mislead. Imagining and creating are thus not superior or inferior ways of knowing to perceiving, remembering and reasoning for they are not ways of knowing at all.'[9]

Poets may perceive more than most other men, may communicate more of what they perceive, and make original (imaginative) constructions out of it. But the imagination is no super intellectual telescope for perceiving more than perception itself! Dr MacDonald conceded that imagining sometimes helps one to *gain* knowledge, through 'hypotheses, theories, diagrams'. But what is so imagined requires to be confirmed by perception, and then is no longer known 'by imagination'.

This is on the whole true; although ordinary use is, I think, slightly more hospitable to quasi-perceptual senses of 'imagine' and its cognates than Dr MacDonald suggests. If I enter a dimly lit room I may imagine that what is in fact a couch is a crouching burglar. 'I imagined wrongly', 'I was misled by my imagination' are surely legitimate ways of describing my mistake. But confirmation, certainly, comes not by further imaginings but by turning up the lights and removing the perceptual ambiguity.

---

[8] T. S. Eliot, *Essay on Dante*, 1950.
[9] Margaret MacDonald, *Proceedings of the Aristotelian Society* (Vol. LIII, 1952–3), p. 226.

Even if we were to accept a chastened account of the rôle of imagination in poetry, this would not be to deny it all but the most trivial functions. Far from it: for ambiguous situations (of which the couch/burglar situation was a simple example) can occur on a much more grandiose scale, and confirmation of the 'reports' of imagination in their case are often long-delayed or impossible altogether. In the most general terms, the elements of human experience lend themselves to an indefinite number of alternative groupings, interpretations, slants—between which discrimination on empirical grounds is often unattainable—as if we had to live with the couch/burglar situation *without* being able to switch on the light or reach out a hand to touch. Or in some cases again, empirical confirmation of one alternative may be *in principle* impossible, as it is with the ambiguous drawing of the psychologists which may with equal propriety be seen as a duck or a rabbit. The drawing is *irreducibly* ambiguous; and this through no perceptual inadequacy on the spectator's part.

The imagination of the poet, I suggest, while it communicates no new item of information, may be largely concerned to present one or more of such optional visions of the world, of human life and values; and often the word of imagination is necessarily the *last* word—not always the last word through *logical* necessity, but sometimes through the practical limits to empirical confirmation.

Would this mean that the poet's claims to 'truth' and 'insight' would have to be abandoned? In many cases, no. Some kinds of insight, for instance, do not depend on the receipt of new information, but on seeing unnoticed implications in what was already known. The hard facts were there, but the mixture required to be jolted before the reaction could take place. Swann, in Proust's novel, knew what it was for a man to 'keep' a mistress. He knew also that 'if he were to refrain from giving Odette a diamond necklace for which she longed, he would be letting her admiration for his generosity decline ... Then suddenly he asked himself whether that was not precisely what was implied by "keeping" a woman'.[10] Imagination reorientates the old facts; 'insight' is made possible. If imagination has not *discovered* the truth, it has illumined the familiar premisses from the one viewpoint in which the conclusion can be seen inescapably to follow.

The recipient of *divine* inspiration meditates upon events of his own time and the events of his nation's past, and under the Holy Spirit's guidance, shapes imaginatively rich interpretative images, whereby experiences apprehended in man's finitude may be seen as the redemptive work of the infinite God. But if imagination cannot plausibly be thought of as an instrument of perception, an intellectual telescope, what help can the concept be towards understanding the process of revelation?

(i) Arguing from finite experience to an infinite God as its ground, might be like arguing from the vague, ambiguous shape in the dark sitting-room to a burglar on a couch. The vague shape is what H. H. Price would call 'gappy'; imagination completes the half-seen outline, supplies the hidden portions as best it can. It is important to note that I can imagine the shape to be a burglar only if I have had previous experience of what a man looks like in a crouching position, and to be a couch only if I know what that piece of furniture normally looks like. If I did not know either, then my sentence 'I imagined it was a burglar' (or 'a couch'), would be quite without meaning. So too, if I declare that the object of my imaginative insight is 'God', am I not committed to saying that prior to the particular experience which I am narrating, I was able to give an account of God's nature? Otherwise I should not have known how to complete the gaps in the experience in the way I *did* complete them to yield the verdict 'God is the object of this experience'. That is to say, if historical events or individual experiences are to be made the basis of the claim 'God is revealing himself here', then according to this model of imagination-at-work, the concept 'God' must already be in our possession. But the study of completing the gaps in manifestations of God is usually called 'rational theology'. The strong suggestion is left with us that an

10 Marcel Proust, *Swann's Way*, Vol. II, p.70.

analysis of revelation in terms of imaginative insight once more *presupposes*, and thus cannot be a substitute for, theological accounts of God's nature.

(ii) Imagination does not only complete the 'gaps' in experience; it also dissolves the familiar patterns we make of experience and fashions new patterns, enables us to see the old from new points of view. How far, then, can the questions of God's existence and nature be reduced to questions of the organization, the patterning, of experience, as distinct from the acquisition of new information? Is it plausible to maintain (with R. M. Hare and others[11]) that Christian belief is fundamentally a slant or 'blik' upon the world, unverifiable and unfalsifiable, like, for instance, our trust in nature's continued uniformity?

First of all, the experience of 'conversion' *can* be described in part at least as a massive reorientation of this kind. The convert claims to see the old world in a most exciting new way. But, as I emphasized in Chapter III, his conversion also involves assenting to certain belief-propositions—of different logical types, but some of which in the case of Christianity are irreducibly *historical*. What is historically true might logically have been other than it was; is in principle falsifiable ('Jesus might have been alive when taken down from the cross', etc.). With these the analysis in terms of 'slant' is not satisfactory.

Secondly, it is hard to see how God's 'transcendence' could be recognized by such an account. A painter might say of his painting, 'Follow the line of this cloud, the curve of this hill and the footpath which continues it, and you see how the whole composition is built out of a great ellipse. Once that is seen, you will quickly notice numerous smaller ellipses repeating the main design in other portions of the canvas'. Here is a plain invitation to organize our visual field in a special way. The 'lines' which the painter points out are not 'evidence for' his claim about the composition; they are part of the composition itself. But the situation is very different

[11] R. M. Hare, in *New Essays in Philosophical Theology*, Ed. A. Flew and A. MacIntyre (SCM Press 1955), pp. 99 ff.

when we attempt to organize our experience so as to justify the claim 'There exists an all-good and all-powerful transcendent Deity'. For unless we are content with a pantheism, we are precluded from speaking as the painter speaks; what we point out about the world, the 'designs' or 'design', the beauty or incompleteness, can never rise above the level of 'evidence for', cannot be identified with elements in the Deity himself. And if we are bound to the evidential level, then some sort of inference is presumably required before the conclusion 'God exists' can be reached. Imagination can perhaps provide the grouping of experience which renders the inference most plausible, but it does not seem able to complete the argument itself. As before, we seem thrown back upon those much-criticized inference-patterns belonging to the 'cosmological', and 'teleological' arguments and their variants. If these fail, imagination cannot do their work for them.

The phrase 'imaginative insight' can be used in yet another sense. It can be applied to what has been believed at a bare, conceptual level, but never before 'realized', 'existentially' understood. We have been like the prisoner released who murmurs 'I am free', but has not yet, and knows he has not yet, become aware of what his new freedom 'means' to him. 'I know the truth', said Kierkegaard, 'only when it becomes a life in me.' 'Truth . . . is life.'[12]

The poet, it may be ventured, possesses one of the most potent means of enabling people to come to such living awareness, whether of truths so familiar that they had ceased to make any impact on them at all, or of what at a conceptual level seemed beyond their power to 'realize'. There are obvious theological implications here, but they are not logically parallel to those so far discussed. The possibility which confronts us in this case is that the religious poet of to-day (or any century) may be able to show us the 'truth' by making it 'become life' to us, that theological 'nonsense' may through him become poetic sense, and circumvent the philosopher's sceptical worries. And this, of course, is not to

[12] Søren Kierkegaard, *Training in Christianity*, tr. Lowrie (OUP 1941), pp. 201 f.; my italics.

pronounce upon the mode of the original revelation, nor to develop further our Analogy between the poet and the writer to whom revelation is vouchsafed.

The question raised then by this sense of 'imaginative insight' is how the lively poetic communication of a doctrine is related to its truth. Can truth ever be *established* by such 'insight'??—that is above all what we want to know. Certain existentialist analyses of 'truth' suggest that this may be possible. Kierkegaard was so earnestly concerned to denigrate belief which is merely intellectually entertained without being worked into a pattern of life, that he went so far as to *define* 'truth' in terms of passionate commitment. But although in one good sense of 'know', I do not know the truth until it comes alive for me, the converse does not follow, namely that whatever comes to life can be counted on as truth. In particular, the problems of meaning, and thus of possibility, are so grave in Christian apologetics, that if a poet (like Eliot in his *Four Quartets*) should seem to overcome them and to relate Christian beliefs to our ordinary life and language, it is extremely tempting to look on this achievement as a complete vindication of Christianity. Poetry, as Eliot himself has said, can prove that certain worlds of thought and feeling are *possible*; but that, despite phenomenologists who declare the contrary, is not to prove them true. Through the work of the religious poet we may see the world and the human situation in it as if Christianity were true. But, since its truth does not simply consist in a slant on the world, a reorganization of the familiar, that 'as if' cannot be ignored. The reader of a poem must make 'provisional acceptances' (in I. A. Richards' phrase) of a poet's attitude while seeking to appreciate his poem : but success in communication does not by itself justify changing this provisional acceptance to unqualified commitment; although, with a powerful poem, the distinction may be very hard to maintain.

Unless 'truth' is to be used as an honorific title for the impressiveness of what a great poet may show about the Christian symbols—their astonishing comprehensiveness, flexibility, power to evoke the profoundest feeling, we must deny that imaginative insight even on this scale is enough to establish more than meaningfulness and possibility. When these questions are answered, if they *can* be answered, there still remains the question, Is this one *possible* view of things, or is there good reason to believe it not only possible but also *actual*?

No doubt 'truth' has often been used in just this honorific way; and in quite a number of still different ways, in poetical theories. Ambiguity here makes it all too easy to allow unnoticed shifts of meaning to suggest illicitly that if a poem is 'true' in one of these senses, it must be true in some other sense too: if true in sense (i) (showing how the world looks to the Christian), then also true in sense (ii), (giving reason to accept the Christian beliefs as well-grounded). Or, returning to our Analogy, if the poet's activity is truth-achieving, then the 'poems' of revelation may be so too.

'Can a poem be "true"?' Yes, say that if you like; but do not imagine that gives you warrant to go on, 'poems give us true information through "intuition into the hidden nature of things"'. A poem may be 'true' in the sense that it reveals an 'internal necessity', a convincing shapeliness, coherence and economy of materials. A poem may be 'true' in the sense that it is the sincere expression of opinions sincerely held.[13] Or: I may call a poem true if it makes me see a tree as I have never seen it before—not as a provider of shade, a representative of a well-known species or as good or bad for firewood, but in its startling particularity. No hidden features of the tree have been described for the first time; the experience of particularity was available potentially at any time and with regard to almost any tree, real or imaginary. The idea 'tree' has lain in one's mind like (but not *altogether* like) a set of premises ready to yield a conclusion one had never drawn. Not altogether like premises; for there is no inference-procedure here for the logician to formalize.

To see the world (as much as we can of it) in its naked particularity may be a religious experience. 'Not *how* the

[13] On senses of 'true' in poetical criticism, see I. A. Richards, *Principles of Literary Criticism* (Routledge and Kegan Paul 1926), pp. 268 ff.

world is, is the mystical, but *that* it is', said Wittgenstein.[14] But it is only in a weak sense of 'mystical' that this is so, not in the sense in which an awareness of the world's existence furnishes grounds for positing a Being, who is not the world, nor in the world, nor a name for the world's particularity, or the wonder of its existence. And the sense of 'true' in which the poem about the tree was true does not suffice (without the patterns of inference of which we have spoken earlier) to lead us beyond the given elements of experience to a god 'behind' the phenomena.

4. 'ALTERNATIVE WORLDS'

Before leaving the subject of imagination, insight and truth, it may be useful to develop an idea already briefly discussed above, the function of imagination in presenting alternative ways of seeing situations which might be called 'ambiguous'.[15] What is 'given' to perception may often be interpreted in more than one way. We cannot claim that there is a single world common to all percipients who have no option but to interpret it in the same common fashion. To some extent (to exactly *what* extent epistemologists differ) the knower imposes form on what his senses receive: in Ernst Cassirer's words, 'the apparently "given" is seen, on closer analysis, to be already processed by certain acts of either the linguistic, the mythical, or the logico-theoretical "apperception"'.[16] The more freedom of play we allow the imagination in interpreting the given—and in some 'post Kantian' epistemologies this freedom is very considerable—the less easy it is to deny that with equal validity the world may be seen to one man's imagination as godless and to another as God-made and God-maintained. Despite what I have argued above against the idea that belief in God is a 'slant' on the world, a reader

[14] Ludwig Wittgenstein, *Tractatus Logico-Philosophicus* (Routledge and Kegan Paul 1922), 6·44.

[15] Situations of this kind were the subject of a broadcast discussion between Professor A. G. N. Flew and myself (Sept. 1955). This script was reprinted in *The Plain View* (Winter 1955).

[16] Quoted in *The Philosophy of Ernst Cassirer*, Ed. P. A. Schilpp (Evanston 1949), p. 293.

who is impressed by the sort of analysis Cassirer offers may suspect that I have not fully reckoned with the scope of this choice between alternative words.

In the first place, no matter how great the rôle allowed to creativity in knowing, the two concepts—creation and knowledge cannot (logically) be assimilated to one another. We learn to use the two sets of words partly by *contrasting* making things which are not already in existence with knowing things that *are* already there. *All* knowing cannot be creating. The limits of enquiry must be the discovery of the *extent* of our interpretation of the given, the *scope* of ambiguity, the degree of malleability of the world under the imagination. All of this requires a systematic study which this book cannot attempt. The most we can do here is to sample some cases in which the malleability seems greatest, and ask whether we can detect any theological implications which could lead to revision of our previous scepticism over this approach.

(i) The simplest wavy line, says Cassirer, can be multiply ambiguous. It may be seen as a geometrical figure, an aesthetic ornament, a sign, a symbol of certain states of the inner life.[17]

(ii) In *À La Recherche du Temps Perdu*, Marcel sees Robert St Loup's mistress as a prostitute, whereas St Loup sees her as his faithful lover. 'I realized', Marcel muses, 'all that the human imagination can put behind a little scrap of face . . .'[18]

(iii) The different names given by different peoples to the moon—the Measuring One, the Shining One, for example—are not mere optional labels for 'the same object', one common moon. The name determines how the object shall be seen. There are, therefore, as many different concepts of 'moon' as there are names of the kind exemplified. The concept is not 'given' in perception, but is the product of the autonomous activity of the mind.[19]

In his philosophical essays Friedrich Waismann has given vivid instances of how the structure of a language (not only in

---

[17] Ernst Cassirer, *The Philosophy of Symbolic Forms*, III, p. 231.
[18] Marcel Proust, *The Guermantes Way*, I, p. 213.
[19] Ernst Cassirer, *Language and Myth*, p. 31.

its *naming* function) determines the way the world looks to the person who speaks and thinks in it. A language, say, with words describing the *lustre* of coloured objects but with no adjectives for the colours themselves, would force its users to 'see' colour-phenomena quite differently from ourselves.

'Thus the people who use this sort of language would say, "The sea is glittering golden in the sunshine", "The evening clouds glow redly", . . . For them it would not be the *things* that are coloured, rather colour would reside in the lustre as it glows and darkens.'[20]

A language with few or no transitive verbs would evoke a world in which event followed event, normally enough, but without our sense of dynamic activity, of one thing making an impact on another.[21]

These instances are of the greatest philosophical importance, inasmuch as they give reason to believe that what cannot be said in one language (or at least not without violating its ordinary rules) may sometimes be sayable in another, or by unusual manipulation of the original one. Despite the present authority of 'ordinary use', there may remain some sense in speaking of making 'raids on the inarticulate', with T. S. Eliot; Dante may be justified in claiming that 'the tongue cannot completely follow that which the intellect perceives' and that 'the limits of intelligence are wider in thought than in speech'.[22]

But reaction against an empiricism which ignored this malleability of experience under imagination and language must not become extravagant. In each of these cases the limits to freedom of interpretation are easily seen on reflection. *Nothing has been shown to reduce all controversy on 'what there is' to a question of equally justifiable alternative slants.*

(i) The wavy line may be multiply ambiguous, but not limitlessly so. A printer who had to reproduce the line in a printed page might ask the author, 'Is this a hieroglyphic or a

[20] Friedrich Waismann, 'Verifiability' in *Logic and Language I* (Blackwell, 1952), Ed. A. G. N. Flew, pp. 138 f.

[21] 'Analytic-Synthetic', in *Analysis* (October 1952), pp. 1 ff.

[22] Dante, *Convivio* (The Temple Classics), pp. 151 ff.

mathematical diagram?' The author might say impatiently, 'It doesn't matter which, for your purposes; simply copy it'. 'It' is the complex mark on the paper which author and printer alike can see. The ambiguous drawing can be seen as an S or even a W on its side; but *not* as an X or K.

(ii) Marcel and St Loup, for all their diverse imaginative interpretations of Rachel's scrap of face, would both recognize her in the street or in a photograph as the same girl. 'No doubt', said Marcel, 'it was the same thin and narrow face that we saw, Robert and I'.[23]

(iii) The implications carried by the names 'the Measuring One', 'the Shining One' are certainly different, but at full-moon the users of both 'languages' would point unhesitatingly at the same shape in the sky, which they have in common.

The evening clouds glow redly; or, the colour of the evening clouds is red. But in either case, *'red'*—not green or blue. 'I throw the stone' may become 'The stone flies from me'; but to both speakers there is no movement of the stone without my previous association with it and without my arm-movements prior to its flight.

If acceptance of the Christian interpretation of the world is to some extent an imaginative orientation, then it is not a simple 'picture preference' like the psychologist's ambiguous duck/rabbit drawing, nor like the simple couch/burglar situation discussed above. The illustrations which we have just discussed have been aimed at clarifying the way in which 'interpretation' and 'the given' interact in some fields of experience. Can we now in the light of this devise some way of bringing out how in the case of Christian belief these two constituents of knowledge are related? Perhaps the following 'parable' may help.

You are seated in a concert-hall during an evening performance. Your attention wanders and your eye falls on a dim rectangular painting on the opposite wall of the auditorium. Maybe it is not a painting after all; it is so dark and ill-defined a surface that it might well be a window looking out to the night sky. Without much difficulty you can playfully

23 Proust, *loc. cit.*

instruct your imagination to see it first as the one and then as the other. From your seat the rectangle is inescapably ambiguous. But you know perfectly well that it is in fact *either* a painting *or* a window and that when at an interval you can cross the hall and look closer you will be unable to go on saying 'it's ambiguous: you can see it whichever way you please'. Unlike the duck/rabbit, one of the interpretations can be verified and the other falsified.

A small change in illumination in the hall may bring the answer while you are still seated. The outline of a painting is perhaps faintly revealed. As the light increases in strength, so increases the probability that one 'preference' is correct and the other false: until, although you may still see why you were originally able to see it as a window, you now need to think away (with growing difficulty) the interpretation which you feel surer and surer is right. 'To the eye of faith, it may still be seen as a window.' This now has an oddly dishonest ring.

Setting down bluntly the implications of the parable, I should say: first, there is considerable room for alternative interpretations of some features of our experience in which Christianity is specially interested. I am sometimes at least free to see my pain as pointless deprivation or as salutary discipline; to see my fellow-men as 'brothers for whom Christ died', or as unredeemed Yahoos; to see a hillside as a site for a gun-emplacement or as clad in numinous glory. But the phenomena are often less pliant. I cannot choose to see the Resurrection of Jesus as either the divine vindication of his Person and mission, or as an illusion of pious imagination—*unless*, that is, such ambiguity is the conclusion of historical study, unless the balance of probability does in fact swing evenly. The historian alone can tell me if this is so: and I cannot expect his answer to be the same at each stage of his continuing research. If historically the probability was against the Christian interpretation, to appeal to 'the eye of faith' on behalf of the less probable view would smack of the dishonesty touched on in the parable, falsifying a non-ambiguous situation by making it seem in fact ambiguous.

It is no avail appealing to the malleability of experience under the imagination in cases where you can *not* equally plausibly have it both ways; not at least without acknowledging that the odds are against your preference.

The moral of all this is much the same as our conclusion about typology and related studies. The theologian who despairs of 'prose' apologetics and is baffled by the wavering uncertainty of historical criticism, is eager to discover how far the imagination can do what these seem unable to do, and how far the image can take over the work of abstract concepts (which produce philosopher's nonsense) and of biblical narrative (which may be historically suspect). In each case he is tempted to over-estimate the analogies between imagining and perceiving, and the degree to which the subject-matter of Christianity can be reduced to an imaginative orientation or organization of experience. In each case, too, some valuable insights are obtained by the way, concerning the logics both of poetical theory and of theology.

V

IMAGES AND THE INTEGRATION OF LIFE

1. THE STRUGGLE TO 'UNIFY'

In discussing the activity of imagination we used as an expository device Coleridge's twofold account—imagination as creative and as cognitive. Coleridge also believed that imagination 'struggles to idealize and to unify', to give shape to the shapeless, to articulate a poem, a landscape or an entire life. The present chapter will attempt to analyse these notions of unity, coherence and integration, ideas which play an obviously important part both in poetry and religious belief. Coherence and organic unity have already been introduced (in Chapter II) as features of the biblical 'poetry' brought out well by the theology of images. But there we said little more than that the coherence of image with image throughout the Scriptures, while it was aesthetically impressive, was of dubious value in establishing Christianity's truth. But though I think this is so it cannot be the last word on these themes.

'Coherence' and 'integration' are not here being used in their logical (minimal) sense of 'self-consistency', 'absence of contradiction'. To say of a drama that it is beautifully coherent, that its materials are well-integrated into a convincing unity, is to say among other things that in this play no sub-plots or characters are introduced unless they have a bearing on the working-out of the principal themes. It is to say that its ideas, symbols, images are closely interrelated (like, for instance the imagery of fire and darkness in *Macbeth*), that the whole is tightly patterned, not sprawling and amorphous. What is commendable in a play is, in this case, also commendable in a poem. Indeed it is within a poem, even a short lyric, that we look for a greater degree of integra-

128

tion than in any other literary form. A considerable part of the delight produced by a great poem comes from its power to enable the reader to integrate the elements in his own experience as the poet has integrated *his*. With the poet's help he relates the hitherto unrelated, and what were before disparate brute facts become indispensable parts of an intelligible pattern.

With some simple translation of vocabulary, the same kind of integration can be recognized as one of the main objectives of the Christian life. The sacramental view of nature is a refusal to see the furniture of the universe as a heap of *mere things*. The discipline of the spiritual life imposes order upon the flux of passing time through cycles of meditation, prayer and praise, under the large-scale rhythm of the Christian Year.

Religious *poetry*, therefore, is, so to speak, *doubly* integrated. The Christian symbols effect their own patterning of a life which receives them, and the poet adds his own further shaping as he incorporates them into his closely unified poem. This reinforcement of one integrating agent by another brings a complexity to any study of the religious poet's work. We shall have to keep it in mind.

Why should integration be so eagerly sought after? What effect does it have upon the person who in some measure achieves it, through poetry, drama or religious belief? Its effect is to rescue him from the nightmare of seeing life as 'one thing after another' and from the accompanying sense of being a passive spectator of a flux of events, which can be neither comprehended nor controlled.

Autobiographies (like those, for instance, of G. K. Chesterton, Edwin Muir and Arthur Koestler) can show their authors striving to 'make sense of what happens' to them, to retain the initiative even where all initiative seems snatched away, by fashioning from certain items of their experience symbols which can give a measure of unity to the rest of it. We see often the failure of the 'pre-fabricated' patterns for a human life—the 'success-story', a conventional division of life into 'childhood years', 'schooldays', 'growing up' and the rest, and the hewing out of patterns which do less violation to life as it is lived.[1] Above all (and here is the point at which the quest for interpretative symbols becomes an overtly religious one) the ideal aim is the total transformation of a life's 'happenings' from a 'meaningless' succession of events into a purposive, coherent movement, we might dare to say 'pilgrimage', and simultaneously to 'personalise' the external world—to exchange a universe which is a vast, bleak, indifferent mass over against one for a universe pregnant with symbols of personal existence. To quote Coleridge once more, imagination seeks 'to make the external internal, the internal, external, to make nature thought, and thought nature'.[2]

It is in the context of this kind of endeavour that the phrase 'the meaning of life' can most readily be given sense. Meaning is not found in life as it is in the use of a language; it does not lie 'there' in the life as the meaning lies 'there' in the words on a page. Rather, it is the *giving* of pattern, the reduction of multiplicity to a manageable form, the finding of symbols, motifs, schemes of articulating space and (especially) time. We say that life has lost its meaning when the patterns we rely upon cannot cope with recalcitrant events, when initiative has finally been replaced by passivity. A measure of the adequacy of the patterns themselves is whether in fact passivity is *ever* forced upon those who put their trust in them. A great part of the power of the New Testament lives of Christ, for example, comes from the clarity with which they show how Jesus lost the initiative at no piont even in his Passion. The events never *overwhelmed* him. Even at the moment of arrest there is no note of passivity: *'Rise, let us be going*: behold, he is at hand that doth betray me'.[3]

In other words, symbols vary in power to unify heterogeneous elements of experience. Only a few are adequate to cope with experience which actually threatens the personal

---

[1] Compare John Stuart Mill, who 'never was a boy', and Arthur Koestler, who claims that his adolescence was prolonged well into manhood!

[2] See Basil Willey on this aspect of Coleridge's theory of imagination, *Nineteenth Century Studies* (Chatto & Windus 1950), pp. 19 f.

[3] Matt. 26.46.

existence of whoever invokes them. In tragedy, notably, the poet may try to furnish an image of human suffering which will not only express the fragility of happiness but also fortify the reader to face the worst with a new calm. His image reconciles two ideas which normally exist in the harshest conflict—the idea of the squander of death and of the worth-whileness and dignity of life. Cleanth Brooks has written well of this integrating work of poetry;

'A poem . . . is to be judged·. . . by its character as drama—by its coherence, sensitivity, depth, richness, and tough-mindedness.

. . . Richards' distinction between "poetry of exclusion" and "poetry of inclusion" might be developed into a kind of scale for determining the value of poetry. Low in the scale one would find a rather simple poetry in which the associations of the various elements that go to make up the poem are similar in tone and therefore can be unified under one rather simple attitude. . . . Higher in the scale, one would find poems in which the variety and clash among the elements . . . are sharper. In tragedy, where the clash is at its sharpest . . . one would probably find the highest point in the scale.'[4]

Symbols vary not only in power to assimilate recalcitrant materials, but also in their richness of inter-connections within the total system. Rosemund Tuve describes how the poetry of George Herbert evokes a 'strange sense of endlessly pursuable true analogies . . . which it is one of the greatest of metaphor's powers to awaken'.[5] Herbert, we may note, was using as his image-material the Scriptural typology, some symbols and patterns of which, as Farrer has said, are 'enigmatic by excess of meaning'.[6] To make one's home in such a structure is like exploring a beautifully designed great house. However far you may go from the central hall and staircase, no corridor is without its vista of these, no walk but which finally and graciously returns you to them. The sense quickly and reassuringly arrives—'I know my way about'.

[4] Cleanth Brooks, *The Well Wrought Urn* (Dobson 1948), pp. 229 f.
[5] Rosemund Tuve, *A Reading of George Herbert* (Faber & Faber 1952), p. 68.
[6] Austin Farrer, *St Matthew and St Mark*, p. 11.

The originality of a religious poet like Herbert consists above all in opening up new passages between the symbols, revealing unsuspected relations among them, exulting in their mutual neighbourliness. Thus the disciples abandoning Jesus

. . . leave the starre,
That brought the wise men of the East from farre.

The image-materials are provided by Scripture; but as Rosemund Tuve says, Herbert himself supplies 'the last small linkage' in grouping the dereliction with the contrary symbol of the approaching wise men.[7] The power of meditative verse such as Herbert's is largely due to its making the reader feel that the biblical types are not only being restated but also that their creative life is still producing new enrichment of its own materials, new startling transformations of the familiar, the seemingly 'tamed' and archaic. He feels also that he is *participating* in the life of the symbols; his own life is caught up in theirs; he is not the mere spectator of an exegetical exercise.

We have brought together the integrating aims of the poet and the Christian symbolism. Of both may be said what Brooks said of the poet, that he is

'. . . giving us an insight which . . . at its higher and more serious levels, triumphs over the apparently contradictory and conflicting elements of experience by unifying them into a new pattern.'[8]

These words about the poet may be compared with those of Father Thornton in *Revelation and the Modern World*, speaking of religious belief:

'. . . in its passage through history religion enters into the texture of its human environment in such a way that a single pattern of life is woven out of the various elements through a unifying power which characterizes the religion in question.'[9]

We have tried to bring out the important similarities between the integrating, unifying work of poetic and religious

[7] *A Reading of George Herbert*, p. 65.
[8] *The Well Wrought Urn*, p. 195.
[9] *Revelation and the Modern World*, p. 13.

symbolism. Now, once again, we must try equally hard to bring out the differences. As before, the religious apologist is sorely tempted to conclude too hastily that the poetic Analogy can do more for him than in fact it can. It will not do to say, 'The transforming, redeeming, unifying power of the Christian pattern of life is simply the outworking of a *more* comprehensive, *more* adequate set of symbols than the secular poet commands, but in every way similar in its mode of operation.' This can be shown up as an illicit extension of the Analogy.

Consider, first, two extreme (and probably over-simplified) ways of driving a wedge between the way in which a poem 'unifies' or 'integrates' and the way a religious faith may do so.

(i) The unifying power of poetry, it might be argued, is a poor substitute for the 'real' power of religion to redeem life from purposelessness and chaos. The more one relies on the (faint and deceptive) 'Analogy' between them, the more one advertises one's unbelief.

(ii) The hardening of religious symbols into dogma is an unfortunate attempt to objectivize an essentially aesthetic experience of reconciling discordant attitudes. Religious experience has no more right than lyrical or tragic experience to culminate in a set of affirmations about the nature of the world or the human situation. Only by distorting its logic can it be seen as making truth-claims at all. Indeed, take a religious attitude or emotion as pseudo-science and it becomes *less* available to the would-be believer than before, instead of more so. See the world if you can as the garment of a glorious Being; see men as restless pilgrims whose home is not this earth. Enjoy these visions; let them enrich your total experience of life: but don't go on to say, 'There *is* a Being, who . . . There *exists* a resting-place for the pilgrim, his journey over . . .' The attitude is autonomous; and not all illusion—for it may bring intrinsically valuable stability of being, moral enhancement and aesthetic delight.

In what immediately follows, I shall not make a frontal attack on either of these two outlined positions. Instead, what is inadequate and one-sided in both of them may, I hope, appear best through some scrutiny of those *apparently* simple expressions which they both employ—'unify' and 'reconcile', and the logic of 'attitude'. In the light of this scrutiny, the two extreme views will be briefly discussed to conclude the chapter.

2. THE LANGUAGE OF 'RECONCILIATION'

Our ability to use the words 'unify' and 'reconcile' of a lyric, a tragedy, a religious faith tends to suggest that these notions are unambiguous and logically straightforward. Some examples of their contrasting uses will show that this is misleading.

Note particularly that in certain of the cases reconciliation is achieved only *in response* to some state of affairs; and in others this language of 'response' does not apply. The distinction is crucial.

(*a*) One's attitude towards a friend or lover may be ambivalent. Affection and confidence perhaps are in conflict with mistrust and jealousy. Such a conflict can usually be settled by decisive information concerning the person's behaviour. Cases in which jealousy and suspicion remain after the completest possible vindication are normally classed as pathological. They would remind us of the man who says 'It's a window', when there was no longer an ambiguous situation, and all the evidence pointed to its being a painting. To claim in this first sort of case that questions of belief are irrelevant would be quite misleading. Attitudes are altered *in response* to knowledge of fact.

(*b*) Anxiety in a state of conflict is not, however, always resolved by the elimination of one of the competing factors. With very intractable material a conflict may not be solved but only made manageable, controllable by seeing it honestly as it is, maybe by the provision of a poetic image which in its small compass holds together the warring elements. The symbol does not release the tension, but yet gives some kind of 'command' over the conflict. It makes resignation possible to a greater degree than before, produces a 'distancing' of the conflict that brings a measure of detachment. Such a symbol is that at the end of Yeats' 'The Second Coming', the monster slouching toward Bethlehem to be born, in which are juxtaposed widely conflicting ideas—the horror of the imminent new birth, and the innocent and holy associations of the old.

Whatever value is possessed by this kind of 'unifying' image does *not* depend on its importation of new knowledge of fact into the situation.

(*c*) The same must be said of the unifying, reconciling work of tragedy and other literary modes whose logic is similar. If a tragedy enables us to see moral dignity in the face of death's wastefulness, the level at which its reconciliation is effected is the level of value-assertion. The relation between (i) the decision to give something a certain value and (ii) the actual description of that thing is too complex to discuss in this context. Certainly it is not so rigid as, for instance, logical entailment. A piece of factual knowledge which *prima facie* discredits an evaluation may have quite the opposite effect when considered from a different viewpoint. ('Death cannot simply be said to diminish the stature of humanity, if its imminence evokes greatness like Antigone's or Cleopatra's.') In these cases too reconciliation is not the response to a straightforward piece of factual 'news'.

(*d*) We might helpfully think of a scale from situations where reconciliation comes from 'sitting under brute facts' to situations where the poet's initiative is at its highest, and he has most command over his symbols. Between the extremes lie many intermediate cases: and some cases which seem at first sight to belong at one end, appear on analysis to belong to the other.

Consider the memorable closing image of Eliot's *Four Quartets*:

> '. . . all shall be well and
> All manner of thing shall be well
> When the tongues of flame are in-folded
> Into the crowned knot of fire
> And the fire and the rose are one.'

This extraordinary image gathers up a wealth of symbolic

elements from the poetry gone before: we have read of destructive flames and of pentecostal flames, fire as enemy and the refining purgatorial fire: we have read of 'rose-garden moments', those sudden visitations of grace. And here in one image Eliot unites them all—in an image which itself symbolizes the very idea of gathering up, 'infolding', of unifying and reconciling all that has been in conflict throughout the sequence of poems. The flames become rose-petals and curve in upon one another in final beatitude.

Where on our scale are we to place such an image? We are strongly tempted to say that the poet is in command, as in (*b*). He has brought his symbols together and metamorphosed the opposing elements. But this will not do. Eliot is not merely manipulating his symbols, forcing his petals to meet. They meet, in fact, only if poet and reader are at one in their belief that the world is such that they *may* meet. The lines would strike us quite differently if Eliot meant to act out in them a *ballet of symbols* without reference beyond the ballet itself. The poet is not in such command of this material as we were tempted to think. His image is not self-authenticating. Its extreme beauty and integrating power must not lead the reader to imagine that its *extra*-poetic truth has been established, that the integrative power of the poetry is pragmatic proof of the truth of what it expresses. If God does not exist, or if his nature is other than Christianity paints it, then the flame and the rose will *not* be one, and the most potent alchemy of images cannot make them one. We are unexpectedly forced to conclude that the reconciliation approaches type (*a*) far more nearly than (*b*) or (*c*), for matters of fact (theological fact, not completely reducible to 'attitude' or 'slant') are inescapably relevant. To fail to see this is to confuse two quite distinct senses of 'unify', 'integrate'. (i) Eliot integrates, unifies the multifarious symbolic materials of his poem more tightly, more skilfully than any other religious poet of our time. This is a critical judgment, which I think could be defended. (ii) The reconciliation of symbols at the close of the poem faithfully expresses a reconciliation which takes place (or shall take place) in the world. Eliot is not rendering bearable the unresolvable conflicts of our experience by furnishing an image which holds them at arm's length and helps us to cope with them with greater detachment and resignation : he is claiming that the conflicts *shall* be resolved, and his image is an image of their resolution.

3. THE LIMITS OF POETIC 'RECONCILIATION'

From this discussion we can conclude that the ways in which the poetic image and the religious belief can unify and integrate elements of experience run parallel for some distance but diverge at important points, so as to make the Analogy again less serviceable than we might have hoped. Both seek to give unity of being, to redeem life from 'meaninglessness'; but the Christian reconciliation comes about through response to 'information' about the world, which may provide an admirable subject-matter for poetry but cannot be itself *established* poetically. Here the reconciliation within poetry depends on a prior extra-poetic reconciliation.

At the end of section one of this chapter, I referred to two extreme and opposite ways in which similarity between the power of poetry and religion to integrate might be denied. The vocabulary of 'reconcile' and 'attitude' should now have been sufficiently clarified to make plain the inadequacy of both.

(i) 'The unifying power of poetry is a poor substitute for the "real" power of religion to redeem life. . . .' This is true, in that it recognizes the inevitable divergence between their modes of reconciling and unifying; false, in that there is in fact no one 'real' way of unifying life or reconciling conflicts, but, as we have seen, many ways.

(ii) 'The hardening of religious symbols into dogma is an unfortunate attempt to objectivize an essentially aesthetic experience of reconciling discordant attitudes.' Religious attitudes are distorted by being taken as entailing statements about *what is*.

The assumption here is that attitudes may be taken up at will and discarded at will, or at least with some suitable linguistic help. The attitudes are largely autonomous: they cannot be shown to be out of place by appeal to 'states of affairs'. Now this assumption we have found to fail: it fails because it does not reckon with those attitudes which can be taken up only in *response* to states of affairs. If I say 'The Lord is my strength and shield', and if I am a believer, I may experience feelings of exultation and be confirmed in an attitude of quiet confidence. If, however, I tell myself that the arousal of such feelings and confirming of attitude is *the* function of the sentence, that despite appearances it does not refer to a state of affairs, then the more I reflect on this the less I shall exult and the less appropriate my attitude will seem. For there was no magic in the sentence by virtue of which it mediated feelings and confirmed attitudes: these were *responses* to the kind of Being to whom, I trusted, the sentence referred: and response is possible only so long as that exists to which or to whom the response is made.

VI

COSMOLOGICAL AND RELIGIOUS IDEAS, AND THE ANALOGY WITH POETRY

IN the previous four chapters we have discussed the relation between image and historical event, the difficulty of passing from talk about the therapeutic efficacy of archetypes to talk of their objective reference; and have traced some of the complex web of senses in which a poem or revealed image gives 'insight', can be 'true', can integrate the conflicting elements of a life. What has been left to the present chapter is some account of the quite unique difficulties which the philosopher of language finds in the meaningfulness of the religious concepts themselves, difficulties not concerning their mode of inspiration nor their manner of affecting the subject, but concerning the strains put upon language in its religious uses—strains which he fears may altogether rupture the lines of communication between those and its ordinary, standard employment. We shall once again inquire how much help the Analogy will give us, this time in answering a new question. Is the Analogy able to justify theological aberrations from ordinary language, as an extension of normal poetic enterprise—that is, as the wresting of words from their everyday uses, in order to say the otherwise unsayable?

For the sake of providing manageable illustrations for this study, we shall select *cosmological* problems more often than theological ones for analysis. This is simply a device to avoid the additional and overwhelming complexity of the theological concepts. I do not think that this procedure will beg any questions; for the difficulties involved in the cosmological cases reappear along with *new* difficulties in the theological instances. Thus to speak of 'God' is in some way to speak of 'the whole universe' (a cosmological concept) *plus* 'a Being who transcends it' and so on. To speak meaningfully of 'divine creation' is impossible unless it is in some sense meaningful also to speak of 'the beginning of the universe'.[1] If meaning breaks down consistently with the cosmological ideas, the theological ones are unlikely to fare any better at the hands of logical analysis.

Defenders of the meaningfulness of theological language against recent forms of scepticism have tended to take one of two views.

(i) They grant that theological uses of words are 'stretched' away from ordinary senses, but they deny that this stretching amounts in fact to a rupture in meaning. The religious language is semantically intact, though the words are tortured, strained, *almost* broken with the effort to speak literally about God and the cosmos.

(ii) Others deny that this linguistic 'torture' goes on at all, or at least to the extent claimed in (i). When I say 'God loves me', the word 'love' is *not* agonizingly qualified (in order to express the difference between divine and human love) : no, the word is used in its *ordinary* sense. I am letting the human concept of love—together with the enrichments it receives in a parable like the 'Prodigal Son'—be my *symbol* of the divine love, although I have no knowledge whatever of what corresponds in the life of God to love in human experience. I know only that I shall act appropriately in God's world if I behave as before someone who loves me (ordinary sense of 'loves'). For the rest I am agnostic; or rather agnostic save for one thing. For I know also that the symbol I accept is an *authorized* symbol—authorized by revelation. Indeed, revelation is primarily the provision of authorized images appropriate to the hidden and inexpressible nature of God.

---

[1] Space does not permit the discussion of theological approaches which deny (or at least minimize) the close relation between theological and cosmological ideas. For one such presentation, see John Wren-Lewis, 'Modern Philosophy and the Doctrine of the Trinity', *The Philosophical Quarterly*, July 1955, and for another R. B. Braithwaite, *An Empiricist's View of the Nature of Religious Belief* (CUP 1955).

This view is obviously easy to harmonize with a theology of images as described in Chapter II.[2]

If there is a semantic problem for this approach, it lies in a different place from the problem of (i). There is no strain within the concept or image; but, as we shall see, the strain comes when the homely and intelligible images are said to 'refer to', to be 'about' God.

In this chapter I shall first consider what the Analogy can do to give plausibility to (i), and then, finally look at the problems of reference in (ii).

I. SEMANTICALLY 'STRETCHED' LANGUAGE

What one language cannot say, sometimes another can: what the poet cannot express in standard grammar and syntax he expresses by manipulating the old forms in new ways. The poet's linguistic tendency is (in Cleanth Brooks' words) 'disruptive'.

'His terms are continually modifying each other, and thus violating their dictionary meanings.'[3]

This fact is worth reiterating and easy to back up by examples. All the same, it is a very *hard* matter to show at what point poetic stretchings do topple over into nonsense, and at least as hard to answer the same question with religious and theological language, even if the Analogy went some way to justify those stretchings too. Our inquiry may well start with some cases of justifiable linguistic innovation given by Waismann, whose work on language we have already dipped into.

In his articles 'Analytic-Synthetic'[4] Waismann discusses the inadequacy for some purposes of the active-passive dichotomy. 'I think' is often more precisely rendered 'It

---

2 Austin Farrer and Ian Crombie have expressed views of this kind; see for instance Crombie's 'Theology and Falsification', to which reference has already been made.

3 *The Well Wrought Urn*, p. 8.

4 *Analysis*, Vols. 10 ff.

thinks', 'It thinks in me'.[5] 'I write a poem' is even more misleadingly active; rather, a poem 'comes when *it* wills'; 'comes of itself'.[6] We might add a parallel instance from Louis MacNeice's poem, 'Prayer Before Birth':

'I am not yet born; forgive me
For the sins that in me the world shall commit, *my words
when they speak me, my thoughts when they think me,*
my treason engendered by traitors beyond me.'[7]

St Paul may be imagined to have been wrestling with comparable difficulties of mood, when he wrote, '. . . I live; yet not I but Christ liveth in me', and 'Work out your own salvation with fear and trembling. For it is God which worketh in you. . . .'[8] To set these alongside Waismann's cases and my instance from MacNeice brings out well the enormously greater difficulty of judging them as justified or not. It is fairly easy with the non-theological specimens to exhibit by 'talk' the intact moorings with ordinary speech. 'What do you mean, "the poem comes when it wills"? "Poems are not living creatures. . . ." ' I then explain how I cannot produce a poem to order: it can be hurried no more than a child in the womb can be hurried. It is as if it had a life of its own. It comes, not like the memory of my own name and address, but like the name I could not recall until it presented itself suddenly to me, as names do. By varying the metaphors and similes I can reduce the scandal. I embed the new expression in a nest of accepted expressions.

But the Pauline expressions refuse to be domesticated in this way. 'Christ in me' is *not* equivalent to 'the memory of his life and teaching' or 'his influence on me' or 'that in me which most resembles him'; nor are these phrases even stepping-stones which take one within jumping distance of the required sense. Again, the paradox in MacNeice's use of language can be relieved to some extent by paraphrase, though the impact of the terse original will be lost. But remove the paradox from

[5] *Ibid.*, Vol. 13, p. 80, following Lichtenberg.

[6] *Ibid.*, pp. 86 f.

[7] Louis MacNeice, *Collected Poems, 1925–1948* (Faber and Faber), p. 215; my italics.

[8] *Gal.* 2.20; *Phil.* 2.12.

'Work out your own salvation . . . For it is God which worketh in you' and much more is lost than economy and beauty of expression. The theological paradox is justified only if in fact the Christian has good grounds for believing that both the individual's effort and divine grace are required in the effective living of the Christian life, reasons which make it less irrational to retain the paradox of Philippians 2.12 than to relinquish either limb of it or to question these 'good reasons' themselves. The Analogy suggested that religious paradox might be justified after the same manner as paradox in poetry. But it seems on reflection that again a return to the prose of theology is inevitable before we can weigh up the 'reasons', good or bad, for maintaining the paradoxical view.

Take another set of cases of extension in meaning—this time in prepositions. A Waismann example here is the way in which one sees the flicker of a rotating disc 'before' the disc at certain speeds—yet in a strange sense of 'before', which forbids the question 'How many inches before?'[9] Notoriously, the language of religion often uses prepositions in senses very far from the normal: '. . . in whom we live and move . . .', 'by whom all things consist', 'Thou lovedst me before the foundation of the world', '. . . foreordained before the foundation of the world'. These last temporal or quasi-temporal 'befores' may be compared with Waismann's quasi-spatial 'before'. But again, if we do compare them, we see that not only are those prepositions modified so as to exclude the question 'How long before?' (which of course is true), but it is hard to see that anything at all remains of their meaning. For not only *exact* measurement is impossible in 'before the foundation of the world', but it is senseless even to speak of 'vaguely or indeterminately before its foundation'. Obviously, it is not only the preposition which has lost touch with its normal range of uses. It has done so in combination with the phrase 'the foundation of the world'—the world itself being a totality which cannot be spoken about as if it were itself merely one item *in* the world, existing before or after other items.

If these specimens are representative, they seem to warn

9 'Language Strata', in *Logic and Language*, II, pp. 15 f.

us against hoping for smooth transitions from non-theological extensions of meaning to theological ones : for it is ominous that as soon as we explore some of the theological stretchings, we are once more confronted with the very antinomies which an appeal to poetry, or other non-everyday mode of language, was hoped to by-pass. It depends largely on what we know confidently about the elements involved in them whether we can admit the stretching to be necessary or not. In the above examples, the sense of 'Not I, but Christ in me' depends on whether Christ is the kind of being who may properly be said to be 'in' anyone—this the paradox cannot itself tell us ; and 'before the foundation of the world' makes sense only if we can already give meaning to 'the foundation of the world'. If we cannot do this, neither can we tell what force the word 'before' has in that context, nor whether the whole produces sense or nonsense.

But a more general puzzlement remains over what criteria can be appealed to when asking, 'Is this or that extension of meaning justified?' Must we, for instance, rely on the all too elusive sense that the new meanings have been given a home among the family of familiar meanings? Or can we rely on universal acclamation—'That hits it off! It's precisely like that!'? A sense of communicative intimacy with the speaker? But what arbitration is possible when the believer shouts 'New sense justified!' and the sceptic shouts 'Overstretched!'? A philosopher of language might suggest two less vague tests. When faced with a dubious 'stretching', ask (i) Can you find other words for the expression? and (ii) How would you *teach* it? If you can neither find other words nor succeed in teaching the expression, there is little chance of it being in fact meaningful. But though these tests often work admirably in sifting sense from nonsense, they seem to afford little help in the present difficulty over poetic, cosmological and religious language.

(i) Ask the poet to find other words for what he has said in poetry, and he very properly replies, 'There *aren't* other words ; only these ones express what I want to say'. The poet is usually right in this : the nearest we can get to implementing the test in his case is in 'domesticating' his paradoxical and strained senses, knowing that much will be lost in any paraphrase. What the poet claims, the theologian will claim *a fortiori*: and the domesticating problems are infinitely worse with *his* paradoxes.

(ii) As we shall see in some detail shortly, it is perfectly possible to teach someone sentences which are really disguised nonsense, as long as the nonsense-logic is provided with a sufficient number of links with the logic of sense. Thus although meaning may have broken down in the expression 'before all worlds', an appearance of meaning can be given by showing the *direction* in which we are to look for the meaning which finally will elude us. 'Before all worlds' is partly 'cashable' as 'Back, back in time, before X, before Y, before Z . . . before *any*thing'. The series is like a railway-line which smoothly crosses a frontier—the frontier between sense and nonsense. But once a pupil has seen which way the rails run, the expression (and many similar expressions) is quite teachable.

Summing up so far : it is certainly true that some linguistic innovations, violations of ordinary use, are desirable, indeed highly valuable, and do not amount to nonsense. But while some violations are readily justifiable, theological examples once more prove themselves recalcitrant. Attempts to justify them soon stumble over the old intractable problems which our Analogy between poetic and religious language is unable to loosen.

2. THE POETIC HANDLING OF COSMOLOGICAL IDEAS

Our study throughout has been twofold. We have been inquiring first what light is thrown on religious language if it is considered as logically close to the language of poetry; and secondly, from time to time, we have examined the handling of religious ideas by poets themselves such as in *Four Quartets* or Herbert's religious verse, asking here if a poetical treatment of the ideas is more appropriate and successful than the prose of rational theology and can transcend the difficulties the theologian encounters. With the present question of 'stretched senses' in cosmological and religious language, the first approach serves to discredit a total and dogmatic scepticism, but can do little positively to justify metaphysical or religious uses. Nevertheless, the second approach may have something to contribute. Poets have certainly made use of metaphysical and religious concepts in ways which have made these appear most impressively meaningful. Has the context supplied to them by the poet, the preparation given to the expressions concerned within the poem, have these actually overcome the difficulties in communication, really made sense of expressions nonsensical in prose, or produced only an illusion of meaning?

Let us test this possibility with respect to a group of related cosmological ideas—phrases such as 'outside (or beyond) the universe', and, for a temporal counterpart, 'out of time', 'eternal'. With both these types of expression it is easy to see how problems of meaning arise. If the universe is infinite, then there can be *no* meaning to 'outside' it, or 'beyond' it. If it is finite, to be 'outside the universe' is presumably to be *somewhere*, and if the 'universe' is 'all that there is', wherever this point is, it must be *within* the universe and not 'outside' it after all. In other words, 'outside', 'inside' are given meaning in the language from being applied to items within the universe. Apply them to the universe as a whole, and they at once lose their bearings. With 'eternity' language, the problem is to characterize a mode of being which (in order to 'be' at all) must have some sort of persistence, without, however, that persistence involving temporal duration as we know it. Does the 'inconceivability' of this arise simply from the impression such language carries of self contradiction? Or, again, can the poet provide a setting for it, in which its meaningfulness becomes patent?

In his poem called 'Nature' Thomas Traherne tells of his 'secret self', whose vision could go far beyond

'. . . my Sight, whose Sphere
. . . Ran parallel with that of Heven here:
It did encompass & possess Rare Things,

But yet felt more; & on Angelic Wings
Pierc'd throu the Skies immediatly, & sought
For all that could beyond all worlds be thought.'[10]

Of the contemplative he says

'His Mind is higher than the Space
    Abov the Spheres,
    Surmounts all Place.'[11]

These are typical of cases where poets employ all their resources to give a sense of boundaries transcended till no boundaries could remain, of ever greater areas of the world unfolded like a landscape below a climber; until finally the reader is prepared to accept these ultimate synoptic 'alls'— 'beyond all worlds', 'surmounts all Place'. The momentum of the rhythm, the entire unquestioning assurance of the poet about the truth of his vision, suppress and make irreverent philosophers' anxieties. The visionary strangeness, the exhilaration, the high seriousness of the verse are in no sense illusory; but the very success of these makes it easy to imagine that more problems of meaning have been overcome than have been in fact. The poet and his reader may not distinguish a vision of a vast area of the universe from a vision of the *entire* cosmos. But from this it does not follow that the poet has succeeded in giving meaning to what the philosopher had suspected was meaningless. The difficulties have, bluntly, been smothered, not solved; for the gulf between 'an area of the universe'—however large—and 'the whole universe' seems no more bridgeable in verse than in prose. The poet has not 'cashed' for us the 'strong' metaphysical idea we hoped he might; instead, he has cashed what we shall call a 'weak sense' of it—not 'the whole universe' but 'a vast part of the universe'.

The vividness with which the poet realizes these weak senses screens from the reader any linguistic rupture which the strong senses may involve. An illusion is maintained of rich, though mysterious, meaning. There could be no more potent medium for sustaining this illusion than poetry, with its

[10] Thomas Traherne, *Poems of Felicity* (OUP), p. 72.
[11] *Ibid.*, p. 22.

incantatory power, its ability to prevent the raising of questions by the reader which the poet does not choose to be raised within his formally unified whole. A further example may test these claims. We shall choose a poetical treatment of 'eternity' language from Wordsworth's *The Prelude*.

> 'The immeasurable height
> Of woods decaying, never to be decayed,
> The stationary blasts of waterfalls,
> And in the narrow rent at every turn
> Winds thwarting winds, bewildered and forlorn,
> The torrents shooting from the clear blue sky,
> The rocks that muttered close upon our ears,
> Black drizzling crags that spake by the way-side
> As if a voice were in them . . .
> . . . Were all like workings of one mind, the features
> Of the same face, blossoms upon one tree;
> Characters of the great Apocalypse,
> The types and symbols of Eternity,
> Of first, and last, and midst, and without end.'[12]

Two of the images which Wordsworth uses to prepare the way for eternity-language are images of motion within immobility. The woods decay, but are ever the same: the waterfalls are never still and yet retain a constant identity, a constant form. In both we see vicissitude within changelessness. Next, the crags which seem empowered with speech not human, and the impact of the total scene—like 'the workings of one mind' and 'the features of the same face' give a glimpse of a half-heard and half-seen 'Being' undergirding the whole land-scape; no more than a glimpse, for the vague image is immediately damped by the succeeding one—'blossoms upon one tree', and is indeed all the more impressive because of its fleetingness. The 'face' image is again itself one of movement within stability, on a vast numinous scale. At last comes 'Eternity', well prepared by these images of pulsing life against the foil of what abides, tenselessly.

Philosophical perplexity about what these lines express does not impugn their poetical effectiveness. Admitting this

12 Wordsworth, *The Prelude*, Book VI.

to the full, we can still ask whether Wordsworth has 'cashed' the intractable notion of eternity. Unfortunately, 'eternal' means more than 'very long-lasting', even when this is also charged with a religious solemnity and sense of mystery. Philosophical worries only start when we seek to pass from 'immeasurably long' to 'infinitely long' or to '*totum simul*', as we must if we are to speak of 'eternal' in its strong senses. All Wordsworth's images are drawn, as they must be, from features of the *temporal* world we know. To claim that they are types and symbols of what is '*not* temporal' does not settle our fear that in fact we do not know what we are saying in speaking of the 'not temporal' at all, whether literally or in types or symbols.

Nevertheless (a disturbing thought), it is difficult to account for the supreme solemnity which the use of those metaphysical expressions imparts to any utterance in which they appear, without once more appealing to those strong senses that still lurk in the background of their meaning. It may be that these senses (in metaphysics and theology alike) appear meaningful only through misunderstanding their logical grammar, and that a thorough analysis can show that they are actually meaningless. But the illusion of their meaningfulness may be necessary to maintaining the sense of momentousness which even the 'weak' versions carry. In other words, the weak senses may be in some way parasitic upon the 'uncashable' strong senses. They offer, in our examples, a partial cashing of 'whole universe' or 'eternity' language, with the unexpressed belief that the fullest metaphysical senses are themselves meaningful. Thus to deny meaning to 'eternity' in its philosophical appearances must destroy part at least of its poetic effectiveness in weak senses. Instead of the poetic use of an expression restoring what philosophical analysis has ravaged, the reverse may be true. The poetic sense may depend ultimately on the power of the expression to survive philosophical scrutiny. And what has been said about metaphysical language may well apply also to the language of religion and theology.

Putting this in its most cautious and undogmatic form; it is not enough for a philosophical theology to rescue religious language from the *general* charge of being emotive and non-cognitive. This is a relatively easy task. What remains to be done *in detail* and with *individual* religious concepts is to examine the possibility which we have been exemplifying in poetical treatments of cosmological ideas—the possibility that an expression is cashable *in part* but not completely enough for the concept to be thoroughly meaningful; to discriminate between weak and strong senses in crucial terms like 'divine creation', 'the Kingdom of God'.

The sceptical philosopher of language need not be committed to the view that 'God' is a meaningless expression at any and every level of analysis. He may agree with the theist that the proposition 'The God of the New Testament exists' is incompatible with a proposition like 'There is no place for reverence or wonder'. For the concept is sufficiently meaningful (tends closely enough towards meaning) to have numerous implications drawn from it, of this and many other kinds. The sceptic may perhaps follow the Christian up to the point where he says, God is not only very great, very wise and very good; but deny that he is omnipotent, omniscient and perfect, and possesses all these qualities *necessarily*. Here the sceptic may claim a break-down in meaning: he finds himself unable to pass from the weak senses to the theologically required strong ones, from the concept of God as an 'imaginary focus' of ideals and aspirations to belief in his actuality.

My conclusions had better remain 'cautious and undogmatic'; for the investigation we have been making has taken the form of a sampling of instances of strong and weak senses, from which no general inference can be made about metaphysics or theology as a whole, nor about the treatment of ideas belonging to them in poetry. We have no reason *a priori* to dismiss the possibility of *effective* poetical 'cashing' of such ideas: only, we have not found them where they might have been expected. (Study of the particular instance and not of the general issue is characteristic of contemporary discussion of a number of long-standing problems in philosophy. 'Are there "synthetic *a priori* propositions"?', for example, is yielding only to a painstaking scrutiny of individual claimants to this puzzling logical form.)

The furthest venture in generalization we might permit ourselves is a reflection on the deceptiveness of those expressions which seem *'on the brink of'* being intelligible, but which leave us in the greatest doubt about their intelligibility in fact. The psychologist is familiar with a parallel set of phenomena, which he sometimes nicknames *'presque vu'* experiences; the sense of being *on the brink of* revelation (perhaps under nitrous oxide), when no revelation is in fact communicated; or, if communicated, then is trivial or nonsensical. Under the drug mescaline Aldous Huxley saw the Red Hot Pokers in the garden as 'on the very brink of utterance',[13] although alas they *remained* 'on the brink', and kept their silence.

Certainly, not all *presque vu* experiences are delusive. Suppose that after many such experiences, I finally see how to tackle a mathematical problem; I may say 'Ten minutes ago, when I felt on the brink of discovering the method, I *was* in fact very near the truth'. At the other extreme, think of an imaginative child who in a division sum has stumbled upon a 'repeating' decimal—say 3.333. As he continues dividing, adding threes to his fraction, he feels he is working towards a remote mysterious zone, a journey down a great slipway into an unearthly sea, where all that is in this world irrational acquires rationality. In this case the sense of being 'on the brink of' is, of course, illusory: there is no progress in the calculation, simply the repetition of an identical arithmetical performance. Nor is the philosopher's vicious infinite regress a shaft at the foot of which strange things may be seen, nor a pilgrimage to unseen mountains. The shaft has no end: the only movement of the pilgrimage is a marking time.

The poet, when he makes imaginative use of metaphysical and religious ideas, intensifies our half-belief that they are 'on the way to' having complete sense, and that we are 'on the brink of' understanding them. But this sense is so illusion-prone that it cannot be relied upon to indicate that the

[13] Aldous Huxley, *The Doors of Perception* (Chatto 1954), p. 46.

151

concepts actually are linguistically sound. Independent confirmation or falsification is essential.

3. RELIGIOUS SYMBOLS AND THEIR ORIENTATION

The view now to be discussed very briefly denies that any semantic 'stretching' goes on in the religious employment of language. Words are used in their normal senses; only, when applied to God, are not literal but symbolic or 'parabolic'. The difference between human life and the divine life does not entail that words used of God have to be radically qualified, risking the loss of all their meaning, to fit their new context: they are, on the contrary, insulated against this erosion by the retention of their ordinary sense, and are taken now as revealed, 'authorized' parable.

The theologian who holds this position cannot, however, remain indefinitely long within the circle of image, symbol and parable. The parables are about God and his activity. They have to be *referred*, somehow or other, if they are to be more than a theoretical symbolic apparatus, consistent within itself, but unrelated to the real world. How can this orientating of the symbols be done, particularly if the traditional arguments are not available to take the strain? The symbolic vessel requires a non-symbolic anchor.[14] Where can it be had? To reject the classical arguments is to deny that God is related to the world as cause to effect, as designer to design, as the 'necessary' to the 'contingent'. In what other, more logically respectable, ways *could* he be related to it? Only an answer to this question could throw light on the relation between the symbols and the God to whom they refer, and tell us how the familiar, finite subject-matter of the symbols comes to reveal an infinite, unconditioned God.

Traditional attempts to describe the relation, it has been said, failed because they did not recognize its utter irreducible uniqueness. God cannot be related to his world in the way any two items of that world are related to one another.

---

[14] In their recognition of this need Paul Tillich in his *Systematic Theology* (Nisbet 1953) and Ian Crombie in his paper come into unexpected and interesting agreement.

Therefore none of the general forms of relation, like cause and effect, can do more than point vaguely and inadequately in the direction of the world's actual dependence on God, which is like nothing else in our experience, and for which there can be no general term. The nearest we can go towards characterizing it is to recount the dependence-relations that we *can* describe, annul them all, and hope that they will have made possible the non-linguistic, or 'pre-linguistic' movement of thought that alone can begin to grasp what language cannot state. If we try to communicate what we have grasped, we once more find that the only words available are the wrong words, the misleading words, which transform into linguistic nonsense what previously was pre-linguistic sense. Best leave it at that—no argument for God, no ironing out of the inexpressibility of his relation with the world. In Ian Crombie's words,

'We do not . . . know to what to refer our parables; we know merely that we are to refer them out of our experience, and out of it *in which direction.*'[15]

Now this may well be true. I cannot think what sort of argument could refute it. But it is equally hard to confirm. First, the orientation of the symbols or parables is involving us again in the 'stretched senses' we had hoped to escape; or worse, in pre-linguistic silence. How can we discriminate in such a situation between 'a relation of dependence, but not that of cause and effect, not that of artist or artefact, not . . . not . . . not . . .' and on the other hand—no relation at all? Ostensive definition cannot help, for, since everything in the world is related in this problematic way to God, we can point out nothing which *fails* to exemplify it. There is nothing to contrast it with, as we can contrast the relations 'between' and 'on top of'. Secondly, there is again a grave risk that 'weak' senses of metaphysical ideas may be taken in mistake for 'strong' ones, as in the poetic attempts to express these, discussed above. Suppose I say, The cosmological argument for the existence of God fails in its conceptualized forms.

[15] Crombie, *op. cit.*

Yet, pre-linguistically, I can realize (perhaps in the silence of night under the stars) what the inadequate words hinted at falteringly—God undergirding the world; beyond the flux, something or someone *not* in flux . . . and so on. But how can I be sure that I am doing more than we saw Traherne and Wordsworth doing?—mistaking vastness for totality, imagining I am thinking of 'beyond the phenomena' when I am really thinking of 'more phenomena behind the observable phenomena'? or letting a great, cloudy image (say, of a huge being, upholding like Atlas an enormous but finite world) do my thinking for me, allowing it to stand for the infinite God maintaining the 'contingent' universe, although logical reflection could show me the gulf between the image and what I took it to be an image of? The hard thing is to differentiate between two possible kinds of transition from the pre-linguistic to the linguistic. In one case the transition means falsification, as when I violate the subtle complex (pre-linguistic) impression someone has made on me by pigeon-holing his character in a misleading conventional way. Or, in the other case, expressing what we hitherto 'could not find words for' may reveal that our pre-linguistic notion was muddled and false, warped perhaps by the ghosts of verbal confusions which now are seen clearly in the light of day. So, unfortunately, the privacy and unfalsifiability of pre-linguistic movements of thought in theology cannot guarantee them against possibility of error. To differentiate the reliable from the illusory seems impossible at the pre-linguistic level itself—just as it is impossible to tell 'true' from 'false' inspiration, or discriminate trustworthy experiences of being 'on the brink of' understanding from similarly toned delusive experiences, at the psychological level. But the theologian who holds to the view we have been considering may simply have to accept this fundamental unverifiability in what he asserts: for he cannot move the discussion to any other level without being disloyal, on his own avowal, to his insight.[16]

[16] For a neo-Thomist version of pre-linguistic 'arguments' see Maritain, *The Range of Reason* (Geoffrey Bles 1953), pp. 88 f.

4. AN AGENDA

This study of an Analogy has sought to provide little more than a theologian's *agenda*. Contemporary theology can often be caught looking sidelong at the poet, his critic and interpreter and the language they use. Its concern with imagination and the poetic image need be no 'bolt hole', away from problems which have beaten Christian thought. The Analogy is fruitful, but dangerous when rashly invoked. To make effective use of it, a theologian must know something of how the language of poetry differs from that of prose description; he must come to know in detail what he is claiming when he says that such and such a biblical narrative is 'imaginatively true', 'a profound myth', 'more than historical fact' or when he claims an affinity between the poet and the prophet.

The most general moral of the inquiry is, perhaps, that appeal to the language of poetry, while often rebutting an aggressive scepticism, still cannot *by itself* lead to a defensible apologetic. In no point have we been able to show that ideas which recent philosophical analysis has branded as meaningless regain their meaning in a poetic context like flowers reviving with a change of water. Certainly, poetry can show us why these metaphysical and religious concepts retain their momentousness and solemnity—can bring out their 'metaphysical pathos' in Lovejoy's useful phrase, but this is not the same. The most we can show is that the theologian need not despair of the sense of his expressions on the sole score of their violation of ordinary language. For such deviations are the staple of poetic inventiveness.

Finally, the theologian might profitably examine those crucial 'gaps' to which we have constantly drawn attention and the completion of which would be a notable service to apologetics.

(i) There is the gap between the coherence, and integrating power of biblical images and the truth of their *reference*. Appeal to poetry cannot make the historian's judgments any less vital here.

(ii) A point already recapped—without 'extra-poetic'

reasoning we seem unable to cross the gap between the justification of literary stretchings away from ordinary senses to the full justification of the paradoxes of the language of religion.

(iii) In the same way we find a gap between the realization of 'weak' senses of metaphysical and religious ideas and the establishment of their 'strong' senses as meaningful.

These problems well exemplify how, even at those points where the application of the Analogy seems entirely to fail, its very breakdown serves to draw our attention to places in theology where further study is urgently required.

Aberdeen, 1955

III

THE
LOGICAL STATUS
OF
RELIGIOUS BELIEF

ALASDAIR MACINTYRE

Introductory Note

THIS essay suffers from having been written with an eye on current discussion among both philosophers and theologians. Philosophers will therefore find what may seem quite unnecessary expositions of familiar points, and theologians may have a similar experience. I hope that both will bear with this. In particular, the first section recounts the development of philosophical analysis in a way that will perhaps be tedious to those familiar with it and only tantalizing to those unacquainted with these developments. The latter I would refer to the lucid and authoritative account given in J. O. Urmson's *Philosophical Analysis* (OUP 1956). If they wish to see earlier attempts at applying the method of philosophical analysis to theological topics they are referred to Prof. J. Wisdom's paper on 'Gods' in *Philosophy and Psychoanalysis* (Blackwell 1953), and to *New Essays in Philosophical Theology* (SCM Press 1955) edited by A. Flew and A. MacIntyre.

I

INTRODUCTION

To undertake an essay in the philosophy of religion that shall attempt to do justice to the contemporary styles of thought in both philosophy and Christian theology is perhaps a rash undertaking. Both disciplines have been transformed in the last fifty years; and the transformation of each has been salutary. Philosophy has never been so rigorous, so productive of clarity, so intellectually illuminating, as since the revolution in method which is associated above all with the name of Wittgenstein. Theology likewise has had its revolution in which the name of Barth has been prominent. But in each case what has been achieved had its roots in a protest against the illicit invasion of one discipline by the other. Idealist metaphysics, that curious blend of philosophy and theology, has left a legacy of mutual suspicion behind it. Since G. E. Moore's return to common-sense as the starting-point and analysis as the method of philosophy, philosophers have urged that it is no part of philosophy to construct a set of speculative beliefs about the universe. Commonly they have gone further than this and argued that philosophy provides grounds for holding any such beliefs to be either false or meaningless. So a general hostility to theological argument has characterized the outlook of most philosophers. 'Theology and Absolute Ethics are two famous subjects which we have realized to have no real objects.'[1] So F. P. Ramsey, the most brilliant of English positivistic philosophers, wrote in 1925. At the same period Karl Barth was arguing that philosophy could afford no access to ultimate truth, that theology must eschew all philosophical foundations

[1] *The Foundations of Mathematics and Other Logical Essays* (Kegan Paul 1931), p. 286.

159

and appeal only to divine revelation. Since then the divorce between theological and philosophical inquiries has become, if anything, more complete, on the part of theologians, but the attitude of philosophers to theology has gradually changed. The reasons for this are to be found in the internal development of philosophy. Contemporary philosophy, as it has changed in itself, has changed in the face that it has presented to theology. These changes can be envisaged as a development through three stages.

The first of these is represented by the movement properly called Logical Positivism. The adherents of this movement for the most part lived and taught in Vienna; the problems from which their discussions began derived from the impact that modern physics had made upon the concepts of the scientist. What emerged clearly in the debates at the birth of relativity physics was that any concept which does not find a place in statements which have experimental or observational verification is vacuous, does not have any reference to anything. So the notion of 'the ether' which found a place in traditional statements of physical theory turned out to be an empty notion, referring to an unobservable entity with no effects of any kind. But a physical entity not physically observable, without physical effects, is a contradiction in terms. The programme of eliminating unobservables from physical theory seemed to promise immense gains in clarity and economy of statement. This programme the philosophers of the Vienna Circle wished to extend into a definition of meaning in general. 'The meaning of a statement is the method of its verification.' To say what a statement means is simply to say what observations or experiments would show it to be true or false. If a statement refers to what is unobservable and outside the scope of experiment, then it has no meaning. This definition was in time modified in various ways. The ban on unobservable entities was accommodated to the occurrence in physics of concepts such as 'electron' which have no observable correlate, which refer to entities that are unobservable in principle. Such concepts are meaningful because, unlike the concept of 'the ether', they occur in theories which, taken as a whole, are verified or falsified by experiment and observation. At the same time the extension of a concept of meaning from physics to language in general raised difficulties in other specialist fields. 'Charles I was executed in 1649' is a statement which is verified by consulting the relevant documents. But the meaning of the statement is not that, if you consult those documents, you will there read that Charles I was executed in 1649. The meaning of the statement is that a particular man lost his head in the past; not that certain words can be read in the future. So that in this case the meaning of a statement cannot be equated with the method of its verification. To deal with this kind of consideration, the Verification Principle was reformulated as 'A statement is meaningful if and only if some sense-experience is relevant to its verification'.

This more flexible attitude to meaning was given its classical statement in A. J. Ayer's *Language, Truth and Logic*. Ayer in that work divides meaningful utterances into three classes. First, there are the statements of logic and mathematics, ultimately tautologous combinations of symbols, whose formal truth is guaranteed by the definition of the symbols employed. Second, there are the factual assertions of science and common-sense, verified or falsified by the relevant sense-experience. And third there are utterances which express emotions and attitudes but have no factual meaning. Into this class fall the statements, or if we accept this view the pseudo-statements, of theology and religion. When a man says 'There is a God', he is expressing an attitude, expressing perhaps feelings of confidence, but he is asserting nothing meaningful. For the logical positivist, therefore, theology was essentially a series of nonsensical locutions.

This simple tripartite view of meaning was gradually abandoned as logical positivism was transformed into the movement that has been roughly denominated Linguistic Analysis or Logical Analysis. It has fallen to this movement to emphasize the variety of forms that human utterance may take. Philosophers have ceased to believe that we can lay down *a priori* standards of meaningfulness which must be satisfied by every utterance. Instead philosophy has become the patient description and classification of all those ways of using language that are of logical importance. The nature and justification of this philosophical method have been ably and amply stated elsewhere: what I have to do here is to outline the changed philosophical attitude to theology. The logical positivists dismissed theology as a whole. Those linguistic analysts who have turned their attention to theology have begun to examine in detail particular religious utterances and theological concepts. This examination of the logic of religious language has gone with a great variety of religious attitudes on the part of the philosophers concerned. Some have been sceptics, others believers. But what their enterprise has had in common is an examination of *particular* religious forms of speech, whether such examination has been presented as part of an argument for or part of an argument against belief. What such examinations may omit is a general consideration of what it means to call a particular assertion or utterance part of a religious belief as distinct from a moral code or a scientific theory. A consideration of this topic is what I wish to undertake in this essay.

The question 'What is a religious belief?' may, however, seem over-general. One of the things that the revival of Christian orthodoxy has helped to emphasize is that there is no such thing as religion, there are only religions. For it is a matter of fact that among the believers in the various religions there is no agreement as to what constitutes an authentic religious utterance. To many, of course, and not the least intelligent and sensitive at that, all religious faiths seem equally untenable. So that there is no agreed criterion or set of agreed criteria by means of which we may define religion as such. The extent of such religious disagreement must in no way be minimized. It is not just that the different religions disagree as to what true statements can be made about God; as Wittgenstein once pointed out they use the word 'God' with radically different meanings. No doubt there are a great many links and resemblances between the various meanings; but there is no authoritative position from which judgment between them can be pronounced. Indeed we find included within 'religion' faiths such as primitive Buddhism which seem to have no concept of deity, and an atheistic belief such as Marxism can sometimes, not without point, be denominated religious.

How then to set about the task of offering a philosophical account of what a religious belief is? First we must pay attention to those paradigms of meaning which contemporary philosophy has found fruitful in analysis in other fields. But if we find those paradigms inadequate we must not let ourselves be tied down by them. Second, we may be misled if we look for a strict analysis of the meaning of individual religious utterances in the form of a sentence by sentence translation of such utterances. For to assume that such analyses are possible is to assume that we can translate such utterances into non-religious terms.[2] Third, because there is no such thing as religion-as-such we must concentrate on one particular faith, even if it is necessary to see it a little in the context of general *Religionsgeschichte*. In this essay I shall be concerned with Christianity.

Before, however, we can proceed to the task of description, we must consider a group of arguments which have had a certain vogue among theologians. These arguments tend to the conclusion that religious language is *totaliter aliter* than other language; that only those who have faith or special religious experiences of some sort can hope to understand it. It would follow from this that the philosopher cannot expect *qua* philosopher to understand it, and the whole point of this essay would be misconceived. But I shall argue in the next section that this point of view itself rests on misconceptions of the nature of religious language, in particular, and indeed of language in general.

---

[2] I have in mind the type of philosophical analysis practised by some of the pupils of Moore and Russell in the nineteen-twenties and early nineteen-thirties. Their method of analysis was to substitute clear and unambiguous sentences for unclear ones, so that philosophy consisted in exhibiting by means of definitions the essential meaning of puzzling utterances. The presupposition of this method appears to have been the belief that complete logical clarity might be achieved in a logically perfect language of which the

outstanding feature would be the names of the simple elements which compose reality. An excellent discussion of this curiously metaphysical view is contained in the late Dr Margaret Macdonald's 'Introduction' in *Philosophy and Analysis* (Blackwell 1954), a collection of papers from the journal *Analysis* which she edited. An attempt to say what logical perfection in language would be is of course the core of Wittgenstein's *Tractatus Logico-Philosophicus* and we owe to Wittgenstein himself, principally, the rejection of this whole approach to philosophy, and the substitution of an attempt to say what any given expression means by setting out the ways in which it is used. But the philosopher is not a mere collector of uses of language: to tell us how as a matter of fact language is used is the task presumably of the philologist and the lexicographer. The philosopher is concerned to show how an expression is used so that it has point and purpose. He is concerned with language as it is used with logical success. So the philosopher's approach to language is both empirical and normative.

To offer a philosophical analysis of religious utterances therefore we must see how they are used in all the complexity and variety of the contexts in which they are used. And to do this is to see at once that what puzzles us about religious language is not so much individual utterances as the whole business of religion and of religious ways of talking. So that even if philosophical considerations did not enter into the matter, a sentence type analysis would not help us. We cannot say what, e.g., 'God loves us' means in isolation. We cannot elucidate it by equivalent statements, for if they are genuinely equivalent they will retain all the features that puzzle us in 'God loves us', and hence not serve as an elucidation. To assume that 'God loves us' could be so elucidated would be to assume that what has puzzled philosophers about religious language, namely its religious character, could be eliminated without doing violence to the meaning of what is said. So to interpret 'God loves us' as meaning 'Hurrah for the universe!' or 'There is a powerful and benevolent Being who will protect us against illness, war and other catastrophes' is to misinterpret by ignoring the fact that 'God loves us' can only be understood correctly in the whole context of religious discourse. To delineate this context is the aim of this essay.

II

IS RELIGIOUS LANGUAGE SO IDIOSYN-CRATIC THAT WE CAN HOPE FOR NO PHILOSOPHICAL ACCOUNT OF IT?

IT would be odd if the answer to this question were 'Yes'. For a great many of the expressions which find a place in religious utterance, in fact the vast majority of such expressions, derive their sense from their use in other and non-religious contexts. To praise, to love, to recount great deeds, to express awe: all these employ expressions which find their place in the fabric of everyday language. Nor does religion confer on such expressions a new and esoteric meaning. That this is so is shown by the insistence of theologians that certain particular expressions should be used in religious utterance, and not others. God is our Father, but not our Mother; loves us, but does not hate us; we are bound to obey him, not defy him; and so on. Father-Mother, love-hate, obey-defy: these conceptual contrasts are transferred with all their familiar meaning into our speech about God. This rather obvious fact at once renders untenable three views of religious utterances which have found favour with certain schools of theologians.

There has been a consistent strain in Protestant theology which has held that meaning is conferred on religious assertions by a special illumination of the believing mind. Certain statements of Karl Barth, for example, seem to suggest that the assertions of the Bible are meaningless to anyone who has not received a special miracle of grace. But to suggest this is to use the word 'meaningless' meaninglessly. For what would it be to confer meaning on an otherwise meaningless expression? Suppose the form of words: 'Mountain neither fire red here'. The syntactical rules of English render this meaningless.

To make it meaningful one would have to provide a set of rules whereby such an expression could be decoded, could be translated into a syntactically recognizable expression. Unless the expression could be decoded it would be meaningless for anyone, whatever their special inner graces; if the expression could be decoded it would be meaningful for anyone, provided only that there was access to the code, to the rules of translation. But for most theological and biblical expressions there is not even a problem of decoding. Because most religious language utilizes familiar words with familiar meanings their sense is equally apparent to believer and unbeliever. Talk about 'the language of the Bible' or 'religious language' must not conceal from us that such language is nothing more nor less than Hebrew or English or what you will, put to a special use. As Sir Edwyn Hoskyns put it, the language of the Holy Spirit is New Testament Greek. So that a special miracle of grace might be bound up with finding the biblical assertions acceptable or important (and *via* 'significant' we sometimes use 'meaningful' to mean 'important') but could not be involved in finding them meaningful.

A variant on this orthodox Protestant view is the liberal Protestant view that religious expressions do indeed have to be decoded since they refer to inner experiences which only some people enjoy, or at least only some people recognize. And on this view only those who have these crucial experiences could hope to decode them. But to say this is simply to commit a mistake that is obvious the moment that one tries to vindicate this view-point by an example. Schleiermacher, for instance, suggests that when we say that God created the world we are really saying something about our inner experience of absolute dependence. But if we use the words 'God created the world' in their ordinary sense then the rules of meaning and syntax in English preclude us from referring by them to any inner experience. We could of course recommend that this expression should be construed in a new way; and no doubt this is what Schleiermacher is in fact doing. But if one wishes to mean something other than what the words mean, taken as they stand, it would seem misleading to use this form of words. Theologians do want to insist on this form of words—for example, in the creeds. Hence it is misleading to suggest that Schleiermacher and orthodox theologians disagree about the meaning of the assertion 'God created the world'; what they really disagree about is whether to say this at all.

The root of the matter is, however, deeper than this. For the suggestion of the liberal theologian that theological expressions have private meaning by referring to private experiences is ruled out by the fact that no expressions can derive their meaning in this way. To have shown this is one of the central achievements of Wittgenstein.[1] For to name our private experiences in such a way that they can be recognized, identified and, if you like, dated is to introduce words which are used according to rules. And a rule is something essentially public, something which can be taught and learned. So words like 'pain' and 'sensation' which refer to private experience, if any words do, are words in public language. It is not that we have private experiences and invent words for them. But we learn the words and find their application in our experience. The language is in a sense prior to—and even, although this could be misleading, in a sense formative of—the experience. This is as true of religious language as of any other. In so far as it refers to private experience, we learn that it does so because the meaning of the expressions can be taught publicly. This is why two believers can discuss their common experiences. If indeed religious expressions referred to private experiences and their meaning was exhausted by such a reference, then no two believers would use the same language—for the experience and the language of each would be private to each—and two believers could never know that their experiences were the same. In fact, believers are able to talk with one another on religious matters—they do so at length; and this is because religious language is no private code, but is at once public and familiar.

There is yet another third way of ignoring this familiar

[1] *Philosophical Investigations* (Blackwell 1953), *passim*, esp. §256–317.

content of religious language. Sceptics sometimes say that religious utterances are nonsensical. Some believers meet this charge by not only admitting, but welcoming it. Religion, they argue, deals essentially with 'what cannot be said'. Writers on mysticism are apt to stress this and some theological writers have suggested a link here between Wittgenstein's aphoristic utterances at the end of the *Tractatus*, such as, 'There is indeed the inexpressible. This *shows* itself; it is the mystical' and what mystics have said about how to experience the divine is to experience something that cannot be put into words. Two points at once suggest themselves. The first is Dr Johnson's on Boehme, 'If Jacob saw the unutterable, Jacob should not have tried to utter it'. Mystical writers tend to say what cannot be said at somewhat inordinate length and it is clear that for them such expressions as 'the unutterable' take on an idiomatic sense in which they are of great use in describing and naming what they have experienced. A sceptic and a mystic who unite in saying, 'To try to speak on these topics is to go beyond the limits of what can be said' mean different things by what they say. But this leads us to another and more important point. Most religious language, as I have already reiterated, is of a thoroughly familiar kind. And, as I have also insisted already, theologians and believers generally want to assert some things, to deny others. But where everything is nonsense, there can be neither assertion nor denial. Where everything is nonsense, one kind of nonsense is as good as another. It is precisely because the theologian must, to preserve his theology, use familiar terms in familiar ways to assert and to deny that he cannot accept any over-all classification of his kind of talk as 'nonsense'.

These theological views of the meaning of religious utterances have been overthrown by considering the large degree of resemblance between religious language and everyday speech. The real difficulties arise when we consider both the resemblances and the differences together. In the Bible men go on journeys, suffer greatly, marry, have children, die, and so on. So far no difficulty. But they go their journeys because God calls them, suffer in spite of God's care, receive their brides and their children at the hand of God, and at death pass in a special sense into God's realm. So with Abraham, with Job, with Jacob and the Maccabeean dead. This reference to God introduces all the difficulty. What is said of God is again familiar enough. God calls, God hears, God provides. But these verbs appear to lack the application which is their justification in non-religious contexts. The name 'Abraham' is used as ordinary proper names are used, and when as subject it is conjoined to descriptive verbs these two are used ordinarily. But the name 'God' is not used to refer to someone who can be seen and heard, as the name 'Abraham' is, and when descriptive verbs are used to state that God's call is heard, it is not ordinary hearing that is meant. Hence all the puzzles. If talk about God is not to be construed at its face value, how is it to be construed?

III

FAITH AND THE VERIFICATION PRINCIPLE

THE obvious philosophical answer would be to refer us to the Verification Principle. For such crucial religious utterances as 'God rules over the world' and 'God loves us' are apparently assertions, and what we learn from the Verification Principle is that to ask what an assertion means, how it is to be construed, is to ask what observations would verify or falsify it. If we make any assertion we declare that some state of affairs is to be found to the exclusion of others. The occurrence of that state of affairs verifies, the occurrence of the excluded states of affairs falsifies our assertion. An assertion which excluded no state of affairs, the maintaining of which was compatible with the happening of anything and everything would not be an assertion at all. So to declare 'Either it will rain to-morrow or it will not' is to assert nothing about what will happen to-morrow. Thus to show that a would-be assertion is unfalsifiable is to show that it succeeds in asserting nothing.

That theological utterances in fact assert nothing, are only pseudo-assertions, is a charge that has been made by a number of contemporary philosophers. For the assertion 'God loves mankind' is apparently compatible with the occurrence of any and every catastrophe to the human race. The believer who catches smallpox does not conclude that God was either unable or unwilling to keep him in good health: he praises God for an opportunity for the exercise of fortitude. If he dies, his believing friends do not say, 'Poor fellow! He thought God loved him, but . . .' They say, 'How good of God to take him to a better place!' If an earthly father allowed, when he could have prevented it, his children's ill-health and early death, we should allow this fact decisively to falsify the assertion that he loved them. Hence when we say that God loves his creatures we must presumably mean something other than human love. But theological orthodoxy wishes to maintain that God loves us in the sense that he neither hates nor disregards us. And 'love' in this cont:ast means just what we mean when we speak of love in human contexts.

Theologians, of course, and theologically minded philosophers have long been aware of this problem under the rubric 'the problem of evil'. They allow that the facts of evil are *prima facie* evidence against the assertion that God cares for us. But they tend to argue that there are a great many more facts which we do not see, in the light of which the facts of evil will be seen to be compatible with the love of God. So Ian Crombie has argued in a paper on 'Theology and Falsification'[1] that 'we do not see all of the picture, and that the parts which we do not see are precisely the parts that determine the design of the whole'. How to get into a position to see enough of the rest of the picture, to decide whether or not evil is really incompatible with the love of God? 'For the Christian the operation of getting into position to decide it is called dying; and though we can all do that, we cannot return to report what we find.' But to argue in this way is unsuccessful in two different ways. First, it suggests that religious belief is a hypothesis which will be confirmed or overthrown after death. But, if this is correct, in this present life religious beliefs could never be anything more than as yet unconfirmed hypotheses, warranting nothing more than a provisional and tentative adherence. But such an adherence is completely uncharacteristic of religious belief. A God who could be believed in in this way would not be the God of Christian theism. For part of the content of Christian belief is that a decisive adherence has to be given to God. So that to hold Christian belief as a hypothesis would be to render it no longer Christian belief. But even if this were not so this view

[1] Reprinted in *New Essays in Philosophical Theology*, edited by Flew and MacIntyre (SCM Press 1955).

would still be open to a fatal objection. For the essential crux that the Verification Principle raises for theistic assertions is not that they are unfalsifiable but that they are either unfalsifiable or false. Either the believer allows that the facts of evil count against his assertion or he does not concede this. If he takes the latter course, his assertions are no longer in a meaningful sense assertions. If he takes the former course, he cannot, as Crombie does, argue that there is only a *prima facie* incompatibility between the assertion 'God loves us' and the facts of evil. For it does not matter how much more of the picture there is to see. What we have seen already is enough to make theism either false or fantastic, if its evidences are of this kind. If we saw a father beat his children or allow them to be beaten beyond any degree that might have a reformative effect or could be a discharge of justice, we should deny that he loved his children in a full sense, no matter what else he did which we perhaps never saw. Incurable cancers, the sufferings of children, earthquake and volcanic destruction: nothing could be experienced which would make the occurrence of these compatible with the assertion, 'There is one who could prevent these things and yet loves the victims'. In the face of this the theologian would do well to abandon any suggestion that his assertions are in any sense connected with the way the world goes, as factual assertions are related to the evidence that is relevant to their verification or falsification. And we ought to note that to the believing mind the facts of evil apparently constitute not evidence against, but a motive for belief.

Wordsworth, for example, passed through some of the central phases of natural religion towards Christian theism. He felt as intensely as any primitive idolater or polytheist the sense of the presences in nature, presences which had for him moral quality and moral power. Sounds were for him—in his early poetry—'The ghostly language of the ancient earth'; in the clouds he saw 'silent faces'. The anthropologist who knew his Wordsworth might make a compelling and sensible contribution to the study of early religion. So in the Lucy Poems all nature salutes her:

172

'The floating clouds their state shall lend
To her; for her the willow bend;
Nor shall she fail to see
Even in the motions of the Storm
Grace that shall mould the Maiden's form
By silent sympathy.'

The storm is as much a minister of grace as the willow. And the experience of what is harsh in nature is what drives Wordsworth into theism—pre-eminently the experience of his brother John's death. If ever a man was a good man in the most simple sense of that abused word it seems to have been John Wordsworth. When he died at sea, William wrote:

'Why have we sympathies that make the best of us so afraid of inflicting pain and sorrow, which yet we see dealt about so lavishly by the supreme governor? . . . Would it not be blasphemy to say that, upon the supposition of the thinking principle being destroyed by death, however inferior we may be to the great Cause and Ruler of things, we have *more of love* in our nature than He has? The thought is monstrous; and yet how to get rid of it, except on the supposition of *another* and a *better world*, I do not see.'

Wordsworth's reaction here is only superficially similar to that of Crombie. He does not invoke belief in a better world to support an already held belief in a good God. He comes to believe in a better world because he encounters just the kind of thing that on the Verificationist view makes against belief in such a God. His change of belief was followed by a return to Anglican observances and in Wordsworth's later poetry we find a typical theistic grappling with the conception of a deity 'out of' and yet 'in' nature:

'. . . on the shape of the unmoving man,
His fixed face and sightless eyes, I look'd
As if admonish'd from another world.'

Wordsworth is in no sense a theologian; but he presents a great deal at the heart of theism. And it is not just that he does not argue for theism because he is a poet. It is rather that he is able to grasp theism in his poetry, because he sees that theism is in no sense a conclusion to an argument, an inference from evidence. And comprehending this is made more difficult by invoking the Verification Principle. What Wordsworth makes clear is that the theistic mind moves from the world to God in a way that cannot be assimilated to patterns of factual argument.

One can grasp this and still be misled about theism by the Verification Principle. Prof. R. B. Braithwaite[2] has argued that because this principle prevents us from interpreting religious statements as statements of fact, or hypotheses—or indeed as necessary truths, guaranteed by the definition of the symbols used in the statement—we ought, taking the meaning of a statement as being the ways in which it is used, to interpret religious assertions as a particular kind of moral assertion. A religious assertion expresses and defines an intention to adhere to a particular policy of action. Not all the assertions of a particular religion need explicitly be concerned with this; but it is the function of any religious system as a whole to express such a policy. What differentiates religious assertions from other kinds of moral assertion is that the moral intention and policy is associated with a group of stories which give the policy imaginative backing. These stories are entertained, as novels are entertained, rather than believed, as historical accounts are believed. 'To assert the whole set of assertions of the Christian religion is both to tell the Christian doctrinal story and to confess allegiance to the Christian way of life.' What is wrong with this account can be brought out by considering the situation of the character Shatov in Dostoevsky's *The Devils*. Shatov has broken with his nihilistic and unbelieving past in the sense that he feels himself on the side of the Orthodox Church in all earthly conflicts, in the sense that he accepts the whole Christian way of behaving and associates with it the Christian stories which he entertains and accepts imaginatively. Shatov accepts everything that Braithwaite includes in religion; but—he

[2] In his Eddington Memorial Lecture *An Empiricist's View of Religious Belief* (CUP 1955). How much I have learned from Prof. Braithwaite's writings will, I hope, appear in various passages in this essay.

does not believe in God. When taxed about his belief he can only stammer 'I want to—I shall believe'. The essential step has still to be taken. And this suggests that Braithwaite—like Schleiermacher—is not telling us what in fact religious assertions mean, but is rather recommending a new meaning for them, a meaning which evacuates them of all their characteristic offence. The Victorians who lost their faith lost precisely the ability to go with integrity beyond something like what Braithwaite asserts. The hero of *Robert Elsmere* appreciated that he had to accept parts of the Christian story —the Gospel narrative, for example, as substantially factual and all of it as true in some sense that excludes rival religious beliefs. On Braithwaite's view there would be no essential reason why Buddhist and Christian beliefs should be mutually exclusive, for one story does not exclude a different account in the way that one assertion excludes another. But Christian orthodoxy has always insisted that rival religious beliefs exclude one another, that the acceptance of Christianity entails, for example, a decisive rejection of Buddhism.

When Shatov is converted it is because his wife returns to him, albeit in a most unpropitious way. Nonetheless Shatov takes this as a sign that there is a God. This theistic view, which we also find in Wordsworth, that certain events are to be received by faith as signs of the hand of God is something else for which no room can be found in Braithwaite's account. For Braithwaite meets the difficulty in connecting religious assertions with what happens in the world by essentially denying that there is any connection. But even if the assertion that in this world God acts should discredit Christian faith to the logician, this assertion remains part of that faith. The philosopher is not concerned *qua* philosopher to offer an account of religion that will make religion appear logically reputable, but only to describe how religious language is in fact used. Until we possess such a description we are not in a position to inquire what kind of justification of religious beliefs would be appropriate to their logical status.

IV

THE RELIGIOUS ATTITUDE

THE description of religious belief that I shall offer will fall into two parts. I shall first attempt to say to what kind of belief the taking up of a religious attitude seems to commit one. Then I shall go on to inquire what kind of justification would be appropriate to such a belief. And in so doing I shall also hope to show what kind of justification of religious beliefs is fundamentally inappropriate.

In a general way the religious attitude has at least two elements to it. The religious believer is committed to the practice of worship in some fairly systematic way. Also he declares that his God acts in the universe. From the myth and ritual of primitive religion to the historical narrations and Eucharistic liturgy of New Testament faith these two elements are found together. But there is a certain tension between them in any theistic faith. For the theist wants to declare in his worship that God is such that nothing adequate can be said about him; but he also wishes to say that God has done this and not that, is like this and not that. How this is so can be best understood by considering how theism emerges from earlier forms of religion. For early man the landscape is full of gods, full that is of actual and potential objects of worship. How he worships it is for the anthropologist to tell us in detail; but before the tree and the spring in some sense of 'before' he kneels and says 'Thou, O God', then within him the primitive sceptic casts his first doubts. He does not say 'Your god does not exist', for to say this to one whose gods have the solidity of trees and streams would be pointless. He says rather 'Your god is not a god', suggests that what is worshipped is an inadequate object of worship. So the worshipper purges his divinity of particularity, tries to remove

176

those points in which his god is less than he might be and ascends to a god of all the trees and all the streams, thence to a pantheon of nature and human nature gods (Poseidon and Aphrodite) until he reaches a god who is the first being of the natural universe, whether Zeus or the Prime Mover. At each stage scepticism drives him on, showing him always that his god is less than he might be so long as he remains an object, *a* being, even if the highest. So at last there comes the great break of the Semitic peoples with any God who is an object; God is detached from nature altogether, is placed outside the world. He is neither this nor that, and we can say of him only what he is not. But the sceptic remains dissatisfied: this God may not be an inadequate object, but that is simply because he is not an object at all. The sceptical charge that God does not exist has been made possible. And *prima facie* to rebut it would be to return to an inadequate view of God as an object. But ignoring this point for the moment we are left with a purely negative conception of God. Even apparently positive assertions may conceal a negative content. To say, for example, that God is one, as Aquinas points out, is not to say how many Gods there are; it is to say that God is not among those things that are countable. Whatever we try to say of God turns out to be something that we must deny to be true of deity. So we get the *Mystical Theology* of the pseudo-Dionysius concluding:

'nor is it darkness, nor is it light, nor error nor truth; nor can affirmation or negation apply to it; for while affirmation or negation are applied to those beings that come next to it, we apply not to it affirmation or negation insomuch as it transcends all affirmation by being the perfect and unique cause of all things, and transcends all negation by the pre-eminence of its simple and absolute nature—free from every limitation and beyond them all'.

At once we get the paradox that a passage which denies that anything can be said about God uses expressions like 'next to', 'cause' and 'perfect' in speaking of God. The theist both denies that anything adequate can be said about God and yet says a great deal. And in what he says positively we get the core of his religion. He worships and praises God not just because of what God is (or rather is not) but because of what God has done. 'We love him because he first loved us.' To give a merely phenomenological account of religious attitudes is to miss religion. For the crux of Hebraic religion at least is an attempt to say that a God who is wholly 'out of' the world nevertheless acts 'in' it.

Yet even although God is believed to act in the world, the worshipper remains systematically reticent about him. This reticence is so fundamental that we must look at the language of worship in somewhat more detail.

In worship we do not talk about God, but to him. We are apt to envisage the relation between religious belief and worship in terms of an intellectualist conception of theory as prior to and directive of practice. Prof. Ryle has shown us how this conception is in general mistaken. Knowing how to perform particular operations does not depend on knowing that particular theoretical principles are to be applied. Similarly we are wrong to conceive of religious practice as the application of religious doctrine. It is not just that as a matter of historical fact the practice of worship precedes the explicit formulation of belief, but that we can worship without being able to say clearly what we believe—Beatrice Webb said her prayers in this way for many years—and that one of the theistic criteria in formulating belief is conformity with the practices and expressions of what are judged to be adequate forms of worship. 'The Catholic faith is this, That we worship . . .' not that we believe. In formulating doctrine we are trying to say what we do when we pray. So the language of liturgy is at the heart of the matter.

That this is so may help to bring out why in theism the tradition of negative theology is so insistently reticent about the object of worship. For the language of worship is itself systematically unclear and reticent about the object of worship. There are five characteristic features of such language which co-operate in producing this effect. First, there is the simple fact already noticed that so much of it is vocative. When you speak to someone it is not normally in place to say very much about them. In petitioning God and thanking him we ascribe to him certain power, but the epithets we bestow on him are rarely descriptive and even more rarely precise in their description. This brings us to the second point. A great many of the epithets that we bestow on God are either gerundive or hover uneasily between the gerundive and the descriptive. 'Great' and 'holy' are obvious examples. 'Great art Thou, O God, and greatly to be praised' is the typical utterance here. Third, we habitually in worship use metaphors which express either what we hope from God or our praise of him, rather than what we suppose him to be like: 'my rock and my fortress' or 'light of light'. Fourth, we suggest rather than state the greatness of God by avowing our devotion and by using metaphors which refer not to God at all but to ourselves as worshippers. 'Behold I have taken upon me to speak unto the Lord, who am but dust and ashes' is the latter; 'We praise Thee, we bless Thee, we worship Thee, we glorify Thee' is the former. And lastly one of the ways of indicating how a particular expression is to be used, one of the ways of making an expression precise, is to say in what kind of situation it may appropriately be used, in what kind of situation it is out of place. But the theist will not allow that there is any situation in which worship is fundamentally inappropriate. Thus there is throughout the language of worship a necessary imprecision about the object of worship. In worship we are concerned with praising God, not with describing him. But of course in worship some assertions are made about God. Of the 'divine dark' worshipped in negative theology we say at least that it is dark and that it is divine. As part of theistic worship it is common for liturgical recitals of what God has said and done to have a place. How are we to characterize such assertions?

The first thing to note about them is that they do not occur as individual and isolated propositions each of which raises a separate issue of acceptance or rejection. They always occur as part of a total narration, in which a dramatic wholeness of vision is presented. So in order to understand religious assertions we must attempt to characterize such narrations.

They are commonly denominated myths, and this is the

word I propose to use, stressing however that the adoption of the word carries no implication as to the truth-value of these accounts. The first point to be made about myths is the Aristotelian one that they have a beginning, a middle and an end. They are stories that is with a plot and a culmination. God figures in them as the predominating character. They may be long or short, refer to many events or to few. As to subject-matter they fall into two classes—those which deal with ostensible happenings outside the history of the human race, such as the creation of the world or the fall of the angels; and those which deal with human happenings, such as the sagas of Abraham and David. How do we understand myths? Exactly as we understand, for example, novels. Every form of utterance that can be used in ordinary discourse may appear in a novel, but, as it were, bracketed. And a great deal of narration may appear in a novel which is ordinary factual narration, about the Jacobites in *Waverley*, for example. But the novel is a total imaginative account, just as the myth is. What makes a novel a novel and not a history is that there occur in them names which are not the names of real people, and the names figure in both the subjects and the predicates of factual assertions. Not that there arises no difficulty about the verifiability of these assertions. We know what it is for Waverley to fall in love, because we know what it is for anyone to fall in love. In myths there occur ordinary factual assertions, about David and Abraham, for example. But it is said in myths that certain things that were done were done by God. How can we construe assertions of this kind? By considering what it would be for these sorts of things to be done by anyone. 'God' occurs in myths as the name of an unknown. And it is a logical characteristic of proper names that they can be intelligibly used without our being able to substitute for them a description of what or whom they refer to.[1] We might note at this point that within the Hebrew

[1] Discussion of the logical status of proper names has of course been widespread ever since Russell's Theory of Descriptions. And what I say in passing here must appear as an unwarranted *obiter dictum*. But to those acquainted with the philosophical discussions I would only plead that a proper discussion of

tradition the word 'god' is used in two ways. Sometimes it is used as a description equivalent to 'the divine' and in this sense it sometimes means 'what is worshipped' and sometimes 'what is worthy of worship'. But it is also used as a name: so it can be said of God (name) that he is 'a great king above all gods' (description). But since the description characterizes by referring to the attitudes of believers, neither name nor description trespass on the reticence of worshipper and negative theologian, even although they figure in positive assertions.

Now a new issue arises. We have spoken of the acceptance or rejection of myths. But with imaginative literature, which is the *genus* in which we have so far placed myths, no such issue arises. Or rather in so far as, for example, an aesthetic issue arises, it is quite different in kind from the issue that is raised by myth, in so far as the myth has religious significance.

The crucial point about myth in a religious sense is that it is concerned with the central situations in human life. Love and death, pain and grief, marriage and birth are as important to myth as they are to poetry—and the connection, of course, is not accidental. Any given myth incorporates an attitude to these themes and to accept a myth is to identify oneself with that attitude and so to make the myth directive of one's behaviour. To accept a sufficiently comprehensive myth is to accept a whole way of living. To talk like this is to lay oneself open to misunderstanding. For one might be taken to mean that a myth provides us with a rule or a code of rules, and if this were so once we had extracted the rules from the myth surely the myth itself might be dispensed with except perhaps as providing an imaginative stimulus to the moral life. So lives of the great capitalists might be used to inculcate the maxim 'Cultivate thrift and study the stock market'. But myths are in fact directive of the moral life just at those points where rules become no longer relevant. At times of social crisis, at ordinary times when some novel situation arises

this topic would have been impossible within the limits of this essay. Those unacquainted with them are referred to the discussion of naming in Bernard Mayo's *The Logic of Personality* (Cape 1952).

there may be no rule to tell us what rules are applicable. At times of personal crisis such as bereavement the question of how we are to face this particular death may be obviously unamenable to formulable rules: for the question is how to take death seriously. Rules may always be the subject of revaluation, as in *Crime and Punishment* both Raskolnikov and Sonia reflectively decide to break, the former with the prohibition of murder, the latter with the prohibition of prostitution. But the one is a criminal and the other a saint because of the attitudes manifested in their rule-breaking. Someone might argue that Dostoievsky is representing Sonia as conforming to the fundamental rule to seek the good of others rather than one's own. But, as Plato continually points out, this rule can have as many meanings as there are conceptions of good. Time and again we have to take up attitudes, make decisions and so on where there is no clear rule and sometimes no rule at all. And these are the situations where moral problems are most urgent. For where there is a clear rule there is no problem. And where there is no problem there is no growth for the moral agent. We are morally made and unmade in those decisions where there is no rule to make the decision for us. It is a question then of fundamental attitudes to the human and non-human worlds, of those attitudes which receive their definition and their illumination in myths. In this sense of course Dostoievsky is as mythological a writer as the author of Job. A myth offers us a picture, offers us a story: to say that we cannot replace the picture or story by rules is merely one consequence of the vital truism that if you attempt to translate a myth, it ceases to be a myth.

To speak of myths as directive of behaviour is not to speak of anything strange or esoteric. Generations of English nonconformists found the shape of the moral life not in any set of commandments, but in *The Pilgrim's Progress*. At the close of that work Bunyan provides a myth about death. He does not offer us a prediction in picturesque guise about an afterlife; it would be equally irrelevant to try and provide evidence for or evidence against what Bunyan says. But in accepting or rejecting what Bunyan says—and to say 'This is "literature" and I can accept it in an aesthetic fashion without raising any other kind of issue' is one way of rejecting it— we accept or reject a whole way of living. For we accept or reject a role, the role perhaps of Christian or of Christiana, which the myth offers to us. *De te fabula narratur*. And a character of this sort is always represented in myth more schematically than would be possible in a novel because here a role is presented which is the role of all sorts and conditions of men.

All this, however, it may be said, leaves the fundamental issue unraised. For it would be possible to make myths directive of one's behaviour without believing that they told one anything about the universe. But the religious believer commits himself in his use of myth to the view that these stories are in some way or other stories about a real being, God, acting in the world that we are acquainted with in ordinary experience. This particular use of myth stands therefore in need of justification, and the need is accentuated by the content of, for instance, the Hebrew-Christian stories. For they include what the myth alleges to be true statements about real people; so that the myth includes factual assertions. It also includes, for example, moral prescriptions. To accept these stories is to commit oneself at once to such various beliefs as that certain statements make up a piece of accurate history (the Gospels, for example), that a certain moral stand-point is valid (the Ten Commandments or the Sermon on the Mount), that certain parts of the story which cannot be construed literally nonetheless have application and are to be received as valid accounts (the Creation narrative) and so on. And all these are to be accepted together bound in a coherent framework of dramatic narrative. Not only however is it specified that all this shall be accepted; even the mode of acceptance is characterized.

The mode in which a set of religious beliefs has to be accepted is characterized partly by the very form of belief, partly by the content of belief. The form of belief itself imposes two requirements on the acceptance of belief. The content of Hebrew-Christian belief imposes two further requirements. First, if it is to be a belief of the kind we have characterized there must be some single cardinal point in terms of which the acceptance or rejection of the whole can be envisaged. Second the acceptance must be of a kind compatible with the practice of worship. Thus it cannot be in any sense a conditional or provisional acceptance, for this would perhaps make it possible to say 'O God, if there is a God, save my soul, if I have one'; but it would not make it possible to worship in the sense already described. Third, the acceptance must be, if it is what the Christian or Hebrew tradition says that is accepted, a matter of free decision. Fourth, the acceptance must be one that can offer some justification of what appears *prima facie* to be nonsense, for example, the giving of imaginative accounts of the creation as in some sense genuine, valid or true accounts.

So the issue of justification is raised. How is religious belief justified, if it is the kind of thing that has been described and if it entails the kind of acceptance that is thus characterized?

V

THE JUSTIFICATION OF THE RELIGIOUS ATTITUDE

WE can rule out at the start one method of justifying religious belief which has traditionally dominated a great deal of the philosophy of religion. This is the method which disregards the rootedness of religious beliefs in the attitude of worship and attempts to exhibit religious beliefs as explanations of why there is a universe and why the universe is as it is. In other words religious belief is presented as having the logical status of an explanatory hypothesis. What is mistaken in this conception?

The first thing to note is that if it were correct no religious belief would in fact be justified. It does not follow from this that religious beliefs are not hypotheses: but at least if they are they are very bad ones. It is the great merit of Hume's *Dialogues on Natural Religion* to have made this point once and for all. To attempt to account for the nature of the universe, for traces of apparent design, for instance, by inferring an infinite being who designed it is both to make an unwarranted inference and to explain nothing. The inference would be unwarranted in any argument that sought to pass from premisses about the universe to a conclusion that there was a God of a certain kind. For either the inference would pose as strict deduction or it would be part of a theoretical explanation. If it were a deduction that was offered, the conclusion would have to be implicit in the premisses. We should already have assumed what we sought to infer. For all deductive arguments are circular: they merely make explicit consequences of what has already been said. But *ex hypothesi* premisses about the universe would contain no reference, explicit or implicit, to God. Hence they could not validly entail any conclusion about God. Suppose, however, instead that we presented the concept of deity as part of a theoretical explanation. Such a concept would then be justifiable if it were theoretically fruitful, as for example the concept of an electron is. A moment's recollection, however, of the fate of the argument from design at Hume's hands will show us how impossible it is to take up this kind of position. For the traditional argument from design, from Aquinas to Paley or even to Tennant, is precisely an attempt to offer the existence of God as a theoretical hypothesis to explain the order and harmony of the universe. But, as Hume points out, the design in the world, if any, is so multifarious, as indeed is the lack of design and harmony, that a great many rival hypotheses might well be entertained in regard to it with an equal amount of probability. Hume for instance suggests that we might account for the world's imperfections by arguing that it is an early botched attempt at world-making; or that we might account for its order by analogy not with mind, but with the structure of vegetables and suppose the universe a vast vegetable. But where there are possible a number of hypotheses between which there can be no way of deciding we are not in fact dealing with genuine hypotheses. The essence of a genuine hypothesis is that it should suggest observations or experiments which will enable us to decide whether a particular phenomenon is to be explained in one way rather than another. Where the phenomenon in question is the universe there are no observations or experiments to be made over and above those observations which suggest the hypothesis. And these as we have seen can suggest many hypotheses. Which, for the reasons stated, is as good as saying that in this kind of matter there can be no hypotheses.

Thus, if religious beliefs are explanatory hypotheses, there can be no justification whatever for continuing to hold them. But in fact to treat religious beliefs as such is to falsify both the kind of belief they are and the way in which they are characteristically held. To begin with the latter: if religious belief was the kind of thing that could be presented as the conclusion of an argument, we should either have too much certitude or too little for the belief in question to be a religious belief. For if we could produce logically cogent arguments we should produce the kind of certitude that leaves no room for decision; where proof is in place, decision is not. We do not decide to accept Euclid's conclusions; we merely look to the rigour of his arguments. If the existence of God were demonstrable we should be as bereft of the possibility of making a free decision to love God as we should be if every utterance of doubt or unbelief was answered by thunder-bolts from heaven. But this kind of free decision is the essence of the Christian religion. So that to argue for religious belief in this way would be to destroy it. Hume's discovery of the fallacies in such arguments is an essential contribution to theology. So too is his demolishing of the view that belief in God is a hypothesis. For if it were, we should have to hold our beliefs as we hold hypotheses, in a provisional and tentative way. This we noted earlier was alien to the whole spirit of religious belief. Having made our decision, we adhere to belief unconditionally, we commit ourselves as completely as one can ever commit oneself to anything.

Not only, however, does the conception of religious beliefs as hypotheses lead us to misdescribe the religious attitude. It leads us also to misdescribe the content of religious belief. For the climax of all such argument as we have considered has traditionally been to establish 'the existence of God'. This concept of God's existence seems to me highly misleading. But in order to see exactly why it is misleading we must turn to consider how in fact religious beliefs are justified.

Here we must first recall what we have already noted that there are such things as religions. There may be no shared content in the great religions, but each has its own procedure for deciding whether a given belief or practice is or is not authentic. Each has a criterion by means of which orthodoxy is determined. And in this sense a belief is justified in a particular religion by referring to that rule by means of which it is determined what is and what is not included in the religion.

Such a rule is strictly analogous to the rule by means of which sovereignty is defined in a political society. Political philosophers in posing the question 'What is sovereignty?' have usually attempted to answer this question by naming the person or body in whom sovereignty is to be said to reside. But essentially where sovereignty resides in my society is always determined by reference to the rule or rules which state what is to count as law. The rule in Great Britain, for example is, roughly 'What the Queen in Parliament says is law'. Such rules, by means of which the sovereign power is defined, are not of course themselves utterances of the Sovereign power. Because they are the ultimate criterion of law, they have no logical justification outside themselves. If Parliament passed an act asserting that what the Queen in Parliament said was law this would do nothing to give the rule of sovereignty more validity than it already possesses. What we mean by an ultimate criterion is precisely that rule which lies at the base of any argument over what the law is, that rule therefore beyond which we cannot go. So it is with the defining rule or rules of a religion. 'The Bible and the Bible only is the religion of Protestants', 'What the Pope defines *ex cathedra* on matters of faith and morals are dogmas which one is obliged to believe' are examples of such rules. By means of them theologians determine what are and what are not valid doctrines and authentic liturgical practices. As the rule of sovereignty may leave considerable scope for lawyers to disagree, so a rule defining where authority is to be found in a religious society may leave plenty of scope for theologians to disagree. Again, the rule being an ultimate criterion is not to be justified by referring to who has uttered it; that the Bible says that the Bible is authoritative, that the Pope defines his own infallibility *de fide et moribus* are in no sense justifications for accepting the Bible or the Pope as authoritative. That there should be this analogy between political sovereignty and religious authority is not of course accidental. For all political societies were once in a sense religious societies and one has only to read Dante to see the theological background to all discussions of sovereignty.

And a political philosopher like Hobbes could be just as aptly labelled a political theologian, more aptly if one considers the tracts of biblical exegesis in *Leviathan*.

Every religion therefore is defined by reference to what it accepts as an authoritative criterion in religious matters. The acceptance or rejection of a religion is thus the acceptance or rejection of such an authority. But now it might be said that one cannot accept on authority what is inherently nonsensical; if someone asserts 'Twas brillig and the slithy toves did gyre' and when asked what this means replies that it must be accepted on authority, none of our difficulties have been removed. What puzzles us for example in the acceptance or rejection of the creation narrative, remains as puzzling as ever when we are told that it is accepted because it is allowed in by the fundamental canonical criteria of the Hebrew-Christian tradition.

If someone claimed to be able to tell us which myths and cosmological pictures we must accept; and to be able furthermore to assure us that although we could not know how it was possible for these to represent a true account of these matters nonetheless we could be certain that they did; how could we accept his claims? Only presumably if we accepted all that he said not because of what he said but because it was he that said it. If the authoritative criterion was uttered by someone who was accepted as completely authoritative we should be able to explain how we came to accept a religion as a whole. But what sort of person would this have to be? It would have to be someone who was given complete authority and, that is to say, who was worshipped. We would have to be able to say before him, 'My lord and my God.' If we were theists believing that God is more than an object in the world, we could only find an authority for theism in one who both accepted allegiance to himself as divine and who declared by his authority that there was more to the divine than himself; who could say both that 'He that hath seen me hath seen the Father' and that 'The Father is greater than I'.

If someone alleges that this is not even a disguised account of the Christian doctrine of the Incarnation, it must be said that this is just to show how essentially this doctrine is bound up with the whole conceptual scheme of Christian theism. And from the logician's point of view the criteria employed in the Christian religion can now be exhibited in a clear schematism. What we say about God we understand in the familiar pictorial senses: we do not derive it from evidence, we recognize that the facts of nature and history do not provide any ground for what we say, yet we say it. Our ground for saying it is that we have the authority of Jesus Christ for saying it: our ground for accepting what he says is what the apostles say about him; our ground for accepting the apostles? Here the argument ends or becomes circular; we either find an ultimate criterion of religious authority, or we refer to the content of what authority says.

Is not all this, it may be protested, so schematic as to miss everything that makes religious belief important to the believer? Certainly, for what makes religion important is its content; whereas what we have been concerned with is the sense in which religious belief might be referred to criteria of meaning and validity, and this is necessarily to exhibit a set of more or less schematic relationships.

At the heart of Christianity we find the concept of authority. But to say this is not to say anything about what is laid down by authority, about the content of religion. We have indeed referred to authority in two senses.[1] In one sense as we have

[1] What I say about authority is liable to misinterpretation in that I may be taken to be smuggling in a theological doctrine under the cover of a logical analysis. I am not here asserting in any way the theological doctrine that a clearly defined authority, such as is notably found in the Church of Rome and is equally notably lacking in the Church of England, is necessary to an effective religion. I am merely asserting that in religious practice there are methods of determining which religious utterances are authentic. These methods operate by referring to criteria. The criteria are thus treated as authoritative. But nothing that I say precludes an appeal to personal religious experience being counted as an appeal to just such a criterion. The rule 'What I came to feel (or see or hear) on such and such an occasion is what I judge theological utterance by' is a common enough criterion. Where one is concerned with the origin of a religious tradition (George Fox, Martin Luther or St Paul) such an appeal to experience is inevitable. For from the original experience the tradition which supplies criteria to later believers is itself defined. I am not of

seen the existence of an authoritative rule or set of rules is a necessary condition of there being a determinate religion. And if we supplement reference to such a rule by saying that a religion is always concerned with how men are to live and with what their fundamental attitudes are to be, we produce as near a satisfactory definition of religion as we are likely to get. For by saying that religion is to be thus formally defined without reference to its content we allow for both theism and polytheism, religions of one God like Islam and of no God like primitive Buddhism, all being counted as religions. Whereas any definition in terms of subject-matter and content would be bound to do violence to ordinary usage by ruling out some religion or other. In the second sense of authority, we refer to a person, not to a rule, and to the authoritative witness to that person by others, in this case to Christ by the church. So, if we wish to expand our elucidation of religious belief in the Christian tradition, it must run something as follows.

When a statement about what God has done or said is made it is to be construed, as has been remarked above, in a familiar pictorial sense. So it is when we say 'God creates', 'God loves' and so on. Part of the meaning of such statements is given ostensively in the Gospel narrative. So we mean by 'the love of God' what we see in the Passion narrative. We do not offer evidence for these statements, we offer authority for them. We point to the state of the world as illustrative of doctrine, but never as evidence for it. So Belsen illustrates a world of original sin, but original sin is not a hypothesis to

course asserting that those who have pre-eminent religious experiences infer their beliefs from their experiences. If they did their inferences would be invalid (see my paper 'Visions' in *New Essays in Philosophical Theology*). The relationship between experience and subsequent belief and behaviour is a non-logical one, resembling the relation between an imperative and obedience to it. So it is characteristic of such experiences, whether through feelings, visions or voices, to present imperatives. And the characteristic religious response is 'Lord, here am I send me'. What is learnt by the original experience may be used to discriminate between subsequent experiences, some being rejected as non-genuine because discordant with the original. But it is always open to a man to make his own experience his authority and so become the founder of his own religion.

account for happenings like Belsen. We justify a particular religious belief by showing its place in the total religious conception; we justify a religious belief as a whole by referring to authority. We accept authority because we discover some point in the world at which we worship, at which we accept the lordship of something not ourselves. We do not worship authority; but we accept authority as defining the worshipful. So someone may discover the possibility of worship in the life of the Reformed churches and accept the Bible as authoritative; or in the Roman church and accept Papal authority.

It is noteworthy that in our account of religion we have nowhere found a place for a point at which a transition can be made from non-religious to religious language. One can accept religion in its own terms or reject it; there is no way of justifying it by translating it into other terms. This is the logical correlative of Barthianism in theology. Religion is justified only by referring to a religious acceptance of authority. And this means, if you like, that religion as a whole lacks any justification. But this in no way reflects on the logical standing of religious beliefs. Of science and morals it can also be said that one can justify particular theories or prescriptions, but that one cannot justify science as a whole in non-scientific, or morals as a whole in non-moral, terms. Every field is defined by reference to certain ultimate criteria. That they are ultimate precludes going beyond them.

One concept in particular has been abused in an attempt to justify religion. It is that which appears as the climax of all speculative argument, such as Hume refuted, namely 'the existence of God'. But this concept of divine existence is of a highly dubious character. Our concept of existence is inexorably linked to our talk about spatio-temporal objects. Even the insight of Frege and Russell that to say that something exists is to say nothing whatsoever about its characteristics presupposes a type of distinction that is appropriately made about objects. So is the mediaeval distinction of essence and existence, the distinction between saying what something is and that it is. When the scholastics came to speak of God they declared that in him essence and existence are not distinct; it would have been clearer to say that the whole concept of existence is inapplicable to God. Prof. J. N. Findlay has argued that because God cannot be thought of both as an adequate object of worship and as *a* particular and therefore limited being we must deny that God exists.[2] Only objects exist and God is not an object. Anselm argued that because God must be conceived of as an adequate object of worship he must be denied nothing and therefore not be denied existence. Put Findlay and Anselm together and we find the one saying that God cannot be said to exist, the other saying that God cannot be said not to exist. The kind of deductive proof that they offer, the kind of proof, that is, which is concerned with the relationship of concepts, only serves to make it clear that the outcome of their arguments is not that God does or does not in fact exist, but that the concepts of existence or non-existence are equally inapplicable to God. To elucidate the notion of God we have already seen that any non-religious concept is inappropriate. And to elucidate it *via* the concept of God's existence is to attempt to elucidate it in just such a way. What is wrong with this concept? First, that it suggests that God is a super-object. And second that for anyone who believed, the assertion of God's existence would be as superfluous as would be the assertion of his beloved's existence by a lover; and for anyone who did not believe the concept could make no sense. Either one speaks from within religious language, as it were: in which case 'God exists' would be a pointless expression; or one speaks from outside: in which case 'God exists' has no determinate meaning. As Kierkegaard puts it: 'God does not think, He creates: God does not exist, He is eternal'.[3] For a God who existed would not be more than an object; and where an object is concerned one cannot choose to believe or to withhold belief. But with God the necessity of decision is ineluctable and central. This brings us back to the question of the mode of religious belief.

2 In 'Can God's Existence be Disproved?' reprinted in *New Essays in Philosophical Theology*.
3 *Concluding Unscientific Postscript*, tr. by Swenson and Lowrie (OUP 1941).

To believe in God resembles not so much believing that something is the case as being engrossed by a passion: Kierkegaard compares the believer to a madman; he might equally have compared him to a lover. Those characteristics of the language of worship which we noticed earlier, its tendency to reticence about the object, its highly metaphorical character, its reference to the plight of the worshipper, all these find their parallels in the poetry of love. The inability of the believer to adopt an abstract, neutral, speculative attitude to his belief resembles the lover's lack of objectivity. There is the same total engagement. But if we compare belief to love it must be not so much to romantic love as to that married love which Kierkegaard distinguishes from romantic love by referring to the resolution and decision that underlie it. To characterize that resolution he has to use religious terms and speak of the eternal; and so we find that our analogy has brought us round full circle. Nevertheless both lover and believer commit themselves and both can only say in part to what they commit themselves.

An activity like worship—or love for that matter—is obviously incapable of justification. The appeal to authority is here at the heart of the matter. Critics of religion like Nietzsche, who have attacked religion because it involves an attitude of obedience and humility to authority, have seen far more clearly the nature of what they were attacking than those who have condemned religious belief for illegitimate speculative conclusions.

Finally we must note that all this does not mean that outside the, so to speak, official religions, experiences of awe, intimations of immortality and the like may not occur. Of course they may, but they only form a path to religious belief in the full sense when they lead to an acceptance of authority. If someone asks what religion is or more particularly what the Christian religion is, the only proper answer is to say: 'Read the Bible'. If a man then asks how he is to accept this, the only possible answer is that he must accept either the Bible itself as authoritative or some other authority such as that of the Church which refers him to the Bible. But of course what will be crucial for his decision will be the content of what he reads. The only apologia for a religion is to describe its content in detail : and then either a man will find himself brought to say 'My Lord and my God' or he will not.

VI

THE QUEST OF THE HISTORICAL JESUS

IT might seem however that since the formal ground for
religious belief is authority and religious statements may
be of different logical types, each type of statement might
have its own justification. Certain of the statements in the
Gospels are presented as parables, for example, others as
historical narration. And for the last two and a half centuries
a basic tenet of most New Testament scholarship has been
that to justify belief in the latter a historical inquiry would
have to be set on foot. If successful, part at least of our belief
would have been converted into an objectively justified
doctrine. So long as such an inquiry is not completed we do
in fact have to deal with a hypothesis. So the argument would
run. It is the argument that has underlain the whole 'quest
of the historical Jesus' which has dominated New Testament
criticism from Reimarus in the early eighteenth century to
Bultman at the present day. And often religious apologists
argue from the substantial credibility of the New Testament
documents just as sceptics in the last century used to argue
from their dubious character. What I want to suggest is that
everything of importance to religious faith is outside the
reach of historical investigation. That, for instance, in asking
whether the Resurrection happened we are not in fact asking
a question which future historical investigation might settle
is apparent if we consider how any evidence that might be
discovered would be assessed. Suppose a document alleging
the Resurrection to be genuine certified by Caiaphas were
discovered: those who at present see the Gospels as fabrication would have the same grounds for seeing in the new
discovery yet another piece of Christian propaganda. Suppose

conversely that a document alleging the Resurrection not to have occurred, certified by the apostles, were discovered. What more probable, Christian scholars would say, than that this kind of anti-Christian forgery should be found? For the rift in belief about the Resurrection goes right back to those who gave the earliest testimony.

Furthermore even if it were allowed that historical evidence could establish that Jesus died and left the tomb three days later, this would only establish a necessary condition for belief in the Resurrection. Christians certainly believe that Jesus died and left the tomb three days later, but this is only part of the belief that God raised Jesus Christ from the dead. To the reference to an act of God historical inquiry is irrelevant. But, it will be said, at least some historical events are alleged: to them surely historical research is relevant. Here we must distinguish two senses of the expression 'historical event'; sometimes we mean 'event to be investigated by historians' and sometimes 'past event'. To believe that a past event happened is usually only reasonable if historical inquiry warrants the belief. But the essence of the New Testament claim, as we have seen, is that certain past events can be part of a religious belief, that is that they can be believed in on authority. And this means that while historical inquiry as to such events would always be legitimate its results are not the ground of belief in any way. That this is so can be understood by considering again the nature of religious belief. Since a belief in an historical event is always a factual belief, it is always provisional in the sense that new evidence as to the facts could always turn up. But religious faith, as we have already argued, is never provisional. Nor do we find Christian believers accepting the Resurrection conditionally or provisionally: the gladness of Easter morning is never a conditional joy. Two points arise from this. The first is that to understand that belief in the Resurrection does not rest on historical grounds is quite different from saying that such a belief is not a belief about history. To believe in the Resurrection is to believe more than that Jesus walked out of the tomb, but it is at least to believe this. Some who have seen the

197

inadequacy of historical grounds for such beliefs have felt compelled thereby to give the belief a non-historical meaning, to make the Resurrection a symbol of human possibility for instance. But while it may act as such a symbol, the belief itself is a belief about history. To interpret it as something else is to use old words to introduce a completely new belief and not a new version of the old. Second, precisely because such beliefs do not rest on historical grounds most Protestant protests at the Dogma of the Assumption, which referred to historical evidence, were completely misplaced. The Roman Catholic who locates authority in the Papacy has the same ground for belief in Resurrection and Assumption. The Protestant who locates it elsewhere has ground for one but not for the other. But the difference is not a difference about history, but about authority.

If we consider how believers do in fact treat historical documents, these arguments will receive confirmation. When it is asked for example why the Church receives the canonical Gospels but not the apocryphal, the answer commonly made by theologians is that, to anyone who reads both, the former will carry an immediate conviction which the latter do not. The latter are full of rather infantile miraculous stories, of pointless displays of power; the former are a portrait of which the Johannine claim that 'we beheld his glory' can not inappropriately be made. But this is to distinguish the two on grounds quite other than historical grounds. It is to look to the effect of each narration on the reader. It does not offer a justification, so much as it looks for a conversion.

This brings out in one particular instance the force of our general argument that to ask for reasons for or a justification of religious belief is not to have understood what religious belief is. We can epitomize what has been said by seeing how from two completely different points of view the same conclusion emerges. First from the standpoint of logic. Every chain of reasons must have an ending. Religious beliefs can in no sense be translated into and cannot be derived from non-religious beliefs. To ask for a justification of a particular religious belief can only be to ask that it be placed in the total context of belief. To ask for a justification of religious belief as a whole is to ask for a something more ultimate than a fundamental conviction. If religious belief was not fundamental, it would not be religion. Since it is, it can have no ulterior justification. Then from the standpoint of theology: suppose religion could be provided with a method of proof. Suppose, for example, as was suggested earlier, that the divine omnipotence was so manifest that whenever anyone denied a Christian doctrine he was at once struck dead by a thunder-bolt. No doubt the conversion of England would ensue with a rapidity undreamt of by the Anglican bishops. But since the Christian faith sees true religion only in a free decision made in faith and love, the religion would by this vindication be destroyed. For all possibility of free choice would have been done away. Any objective justification of belief would have the same effect. Less impressive than thunder-bolts, it would equally eliminate all possibility of a decision of faith. And with that, faith too would have been eliminated.

We ought therefore not to be surprised that to accept religious belief is a matter not of argument but of conversion. Conversion, because there is no logical transition which will take one from unbelief to belief. The transition is not in objective considerations at all, but in the person who comes to believe. There are no logical principles which will make the transition for one. There are no reasons to which one can appeal to evade the burden of decision. And just as for the man who asks for a justification of belief the only thing to be done is to offer a description of what religion is, so the man who has come to believe can only give us his reasons for his believing by relating a segment of his autobiography. It is important to see that the same holds good of unbelief. Because it is logically inappropriate to give reasons for a religious belief this does not of itself provide a reason for not believing. The man who wishes to justify not believing can only describe what religion is and perhaps give us a segment of his autobiography. So it is characteristic of the Christian tradition that among its classics are counted such conversion narratives as

Augustine's and Bunyan's. When one reads such narratives it becomes clear that any experience can provide an occasion for conversion. The relation of experience to faith is in no sense logical. So Shatov in *The Devils* finds the return of his wife an illustration and a decisive illustration of divine providence. So Wordsworth by his brother's death is driven into the Church of England. Only those over-impressed by metaphysics would want to suggest that any logical process is involved.

Conversion is of course at once conversion to a belief and to a way of living. But these are not related as theory is related to practice. Religious morality is not applied religious belief. To believe is to behave differently because it is to see the whole of one's life in a new and different light. It is to see one's individual life in terms of a dramatic framework such as that which the Bible provides. It is to live by a morality, not of rules but of examples. So *The Pilgrim's Progress* provided a moral framework for generations of English non-conformists. And this dramatic wholeness of religion is important. For that a religion provides such a dramatic context for life is one more reason why any given religion has to be accepted or rejected as a whole. The rituals of a religion will epitomize its dramatic content as the whole Christian story is indeed unfolded in the Eucharistic action. And in practice to adhere to a religious society is to participate in its rituals.

To have reached the point, however, where we have seen that it is conversion and not argument by means of which belief is to be achieved, if it is to be achieved, is to see clearly the limits of philosophy in these matters. Theologians often behave as if their natural allies in philosophy were to be found among the metaphysicians, their natural enemies among the more sceptical and positivistic. Nothing could be farther from the truth. Metaphysics might almost be described as a sustained attempt to replace conversion by argument. And to do this would be, as we have seen, entirely destructive of religion. The metaphysician conceives of philosophy as able to construct a set of ultimate beliefs : in so doing he makes the philosopher the rival of the theologian. Worse still, he takes over the theologian's language in order to do this. The religious vocabulary is translated into non-religious terms. God becomes 'the great First Cause'. The positivist by contrast shows the impossibility of what the metaphysician seeks to do by exhibiting the fallacies involved in all metaphysical argument. In so doing he leaves open the possibility of exhibiting religious belief in its own terms. Most positivists have in fact wished to show up religion as yet another nonsensical form of metaphysics; but what they succeeded in doing was to make it clear that religion must not attempt dependence on any philosophy. Belief cannot argue with unbelief: it can only preach to it. When unbelief speaks, it will be as Hume does, to show how religion fails if it is judged by non-religious standards of rationality and to argue that therefore no rational man can accept it. And belief has no logically cogent reply to this. It can only recount the content of its faith and offer the acceptance of its authority. Its voice is a confessional voice like that of Donne when he wrote:

> We thinke that *Paradise* and *Calvarie*,
>   Christ's Crosse, and *Adams* tree, stood in one place;
> Looke, Lord, and finde both *Adams* met in me;
>   As the first *Adams* sweat surrounds my face,
> May the last *Adams* blood my soule embrace.

The man who speaks like this is beyond argument.

INDEX

INDEX OF NAMES